NATURE POWER

In the Spirit of an Okanagan Storyteller

HARRY ROBINSON

Compiled and edited by Wendy Wickwire

Douglas & McIntyre
Vancouver/Toronto

University of Washington Press
Seattle

Copyright © 1992 Wendy Wickwire
92 93 94 95 96 5 4 3 2 1

The royalties from this book will go to a scholarship fund established at
Keremeos Secondary School in Harry Robinson's name.

Douglas & McIntyre
1615 Venables Street
Vancouver, British Columbia V5L 2H1

Published simultaneously in the United States of America by the University
of Washington Press, PO Box 50096, Seattle, Washington 98145-5096

Canadian Cataloguing in Publication Data

Robinson, Harry, 1900–1990.
    Nature power

    ISBN 1-55054-060-2

    1. Okinagan Indians—Legends.   2. Indians of North America—British
Columbia—Legends.   3. Legends—British Columbia.
4. Nature stories.   I. Wickwire, Wendy C.   II. Title.

E99.035R62 1992   398.2'089'979   C92-091462-4

Library of Congress Cataloging-in-Publication

Robinson, Harry, 1900–
    Nature power / Harry Robinson ; compiled and edited by Wendy
Wickwire.
      p.   cm.
    ISBN 0-295-97223-8
    1. Okanagan Indians—Legends.   I. Wickwire, Wendy C.   II. Title.
E99.035R62   1992
398.2'089979—dc20   92-23935
                                                                    CIP

Editing by Barbara Pulling
Design by Barbara Hodgson

Typeset by The Typeworks
Printed and bound in Canada by D. W. Friesen & Sons Ltd.
Printed on acid-free paper ∞

Published with assistance from the British Columbia Heritage Trust

CONTENTS

*This book is dedicated to
Harry Robinson's always-attentive
neighbour, Carrie Allison,
and to his around-the-clock caregivers
in his final years: Colleen, Diane,
Heather and Stella.*

INTRODUCTION

Harry Robinson was a perfectionist. Whether sharpening his knives or keeping a record of births and deaths in his community, Harry carried out his tasks methodically and with great precision. It was his way. Knowing this about him, it was with some apprehension that I put the first copy of his long-awaited book, *Write It on Your Heart*, in my local Vancouver mailbox on November 1, 1989. With even greater nervousness, I approached his bedside in Keremeos a week later.

"It's all right," he said approvingly, "except for one thing."

"What's that?" I asked.

"You said you would put all my stories on a book, but you've left a lot out."

For the next hour, we discussed the logistics of putting his words into print, especially the hundreds of thousands of words that had passed from his lips over many years onto my reel-to-reel tapes. It was just not possible to capture all of his words in one book! This bothered Harry, and so I promised him that day to do my best to get more of his stories into book form.

Nature Power, a collection of Harry's stories about the spiritual relationship between humans and their nature helpers (*shoo-MISH*), is a partial fulfillment of that commitment. Unfortunately, I will never have the pleasure of presenting *Nature Power* to Harry. In the early morning hours of January 25, 1990, scarcely two months after that November visit, Harry died.

Harry had been frail and bedridden for some time, but his round-the-clock home-care workers, Colleen, Heather, Diane and Stella, had described him to me in my regular check-in calls as "comfortable." In the third week of January, however, things changed. It started with an unusual pain in Harry's lower abdomen. Fearing that he might be forced to go into the hospital—an institution he hated—

Harry kept his pain to himself. Only when it had become unbearable did he finally complain. An emergency X-ray undertaken at the local Keremeos health clinic on Wednesday morning revealed that his artificial hip had become dislodged, and by now it was badly infected. Harry died early the next day in his own bed, surrounded by his photos, wall hangings and other precious pieces of memorabilia.

His friends and relatives assembled at Chopaka for his funeral five days later. A great tree had fallen, taking with it roots that extended deep into the Okanagan earth.

TWO WORLDS

I first met Harry Robinson in August 1977 at his home just east of Hedley in the Similkameen Valley. On the surface, our two worlds could not have been more different. Harry was a seventy-six-year-old Okanagan Indian who had been raised in the traditional ways of his people by his mother, Arcell, and her parents, Louise and Joseph Newhmkin, at the small village of Chopaka in the Similkameen Valley. A member of the Lower Similkameen Indian Band (one of five Okanagan bands in southwestern British Columbia), Harry spent his boyhood riding and tending horses, bringing in the cattle, fencing, haying, and visiting rodeos and stampedes. At the age of thirteen he began attending the local school at Cawston, but after five months of walking the six miles there and back, he quit and turned to ranching full-time. Harry married Matilda Johnny, also from Chopaka, in 1924. Although they had no children, they ran a very successful ranching business together. By the early 1970s, Matilda had died and Harry had become too old to run the ranch, and he sold it.

Ranching was Harry's life. "It's kinde important words," he wrote to me, "should be on book."

I get to started feed stock from 2nd jan. 1917 till 1972. 50 years I feed cattle without missed a day in feeding season rain or shine. snowing or Blazirt. sunday's. holirdays. funeral day. any other times I just got to feed cattle feeding seson in winter. from 115 days up to 185 days. just Depend's in weather of winter to feed cattle every day. that is I Been doing for 50 winter's that should worth to be on Book if is not too late. . . .

some more I have done in my days. I use to buy land and sell land.

Buy cattle and sell cattle. Buy horses and sell horses. Buy hay and sell hay. Even I buy dog but no sale for dog. No market. Later on I Buy machinery. one tracto[r] at a time. Big one and one small. 2 tractor's. one farmhand Power hay mower side rack. I put up 120 to 150 tone's of hay all by my self. alone with that machinery in 3-4 weeks. But before I have that machinery I could have 6-7 man's working for me to put up 150 tons of hay in 4-5 weeks but later on I have to sell the machinery one by one at a time till I have it all soled. At one time for a while I have 3 home neer Ashnola just about mile an half aprt and was another home and hay land neer Chopaka. Because I buy place with house and barn and everything and sometimes I sell it same way. House Barn corral everything now by then I have 3 place to work in upper part and one down below. that 30 miles away from this other 3 place is but I work in all 4 place in all year round some times I have a hiert man one or two some times all by my self. (Letter, May 15, 1985)

When I met Harry, Matilda had been dead for about ten years. Alone in his rented bungalow beside the main highway, he had no close neighbours, other than his landlords and good friends Slim and Carrie Allison.

In addition to our fifty-year age difference (I was twenty-seven), I had been raised on the other side of the continent, in small-town Nova Scotia. Growing up in a professional family of Anglo-Scottish ancestry, I had spent the better part of my life in school. But my formal education, especially a degree in music at an Ontario university, had left me cold. The oral music-making with which I had grown up—guitars, fiddles, banjos, accordians and pianos played "by ear" in most households—had no place here. Indeed, "playing by ear" was frowned upon. And so-called "world music," such as the Indonesian gamelan, West African drumming or South Indian percussion, was scarcely mentioned. This vision of culture needed rethinking, and in 1975 I switched to anthropology and "ethnomusicology."

Two years later, Victoria-based anthropologists Randy Bouchard and Dorothy Kennedy offered to introduce me to some elderly Native singers in Vernon and Chase. We left Vancouver early in the morning on August 13 and headed east towards Penticton along the Hope-Princeton Highway. Michael M'Gonigle, my future husband, was also with us. At Hedley we stopped to visit with Harry Robinson, who entertained us all evening with a long story about Old Coyote. After leaving Harry's, we drove on to Vernon and

Chase to see Mary Abel, Aimee August and Adeline Willard, all singers who would later devote many hours of their time to teaching me the ways of their music. During this trip, I experienced a still vital oral culture that bore little relation to anything I had known. Here were songs and stories that were integral to living communities. They were not written and did not require extensive technical skill, yet they were more deeply embedded with meaning than all the classical études and finger exercises of my last ten years.

For the next few years I spent time in B.C.'s southern interior meeting Native singers and sharing their songs. At the same time I discovered the writings of anthropologist/political activist "Jimmy" Teit, a Shetlander who had worked in the same area some sixty years earlier. Wherever I went I carried copies of his handwritten notes, his photographs and his cylinder song recordings.

A FRIENDSHIP

Although Harry was a singer, he could not hear well, making it difficult for him to participate in my music project. He had invited me, however, on that first overnight visit, to come again and stay for as long as I wished. So I did, finding it a refreshing break to sit at Harry's table and listen to a stream of stories. During these visits, we spent our time running errands in Hedley, Keremeos and Penticton. In good weather, we took trips to local landmarks, such as Coyote's rocks, old pit-house sites, rock painting sites or whatever appealed to us. Then, from late afternoon or early evening until midnight, Harry told stories.

Our fullest year together was 1980-81. I had rented a cabin in the Coldwater Valley near Merritt to facilitate my field research on songs. Only an hour from Hedley, I visited Harry regularly. He was in excellent health, so we took many trips together. In January and February we travelled Harry's favourite route south to Omak, in Washington State, where we spent long nights as guests at a sacred winter dance. A few weeks later I picked him up and transported him to my Coldwater cabin, where we spent a week tracking down old friends and relatives in the Nicola Valley. On the long weekend in May, Michael and I took in one of Harry's favourite events, the annual Keremeos rodeo.

In between visits, we wrote letters back and forth, sometimes as often as once a week. Even though writing was not easy for Harry, he enjoyed it, much as he enjoyed his storytelling. "I could not Help it for written a long letter," he wrote to me on one occasion, "because Im storie teller I always have Planty to say." Harry liked letter-writing for other reasons, too. He was a meticulous planner, and he could read and reread, write and rewrite his letters, planning every detail thoroughly. He also believed that letters helped to prevent misunderstandings between friends. In one letter in 1981 he urged me to "take time and figure out. It's better to be a good friend for last 4 years. We should keep that way because one of these days Im going be missing. Im old."

Letters helped Harry fill the void left by Matilda's death. They occupied his time and gave him an outlet for emotions that he would otherwise not express.

> I always Happy when I get a words from you. I don't think I can have any Better friend than you. Your the Best friend I ever known. (Letter, February 28, 1981)

In the summer of 1982, Harry was hospitalized in Penticton for a leg ulcer that had bothered him for some time. Because of his mistrust of the medical staff and his hatred of Western medicine, Harry discharged himself, ordered a taxi and returned to Hedley. He notified us of this in a letter of September 12.

> The hospital is no good for Indian like me. Maybe is all right for some Indians Because they don't know. Got to be in there a long enough to know how bad it is the Hospital. . . . I depend on whiteman doctor for 11 month but they don't do. Today is 9 days since I come out of Hospital. Still the same. My ankle not too Bad but not good. So I thought the chance I have I will switch to my own Indian ways. if the Indian doctor can't do it like the white man doctor, then I will know nothing can be done about it. . . . The Indian doctor is Different than the White doctor. he can do it ones or he can never [do] it ones.

Harry's frustration with hospitals and doctors was partly because he believed *plak* to be the cause of his ulcer.

> They call that "plak" in the Indian word. But in English they call it witchcraft. And they could dig that to the river or to the creek or to the

lake, wherever is water. Go over there and take a bath, you know, early in the morning. After take that, they hold 'em and talk to 'em just like I do now with you. Talk to 'em and then they tell 'em what his wish. He wish for that person to die or he wish for that person to get hurt. But not die. Just get hurt. Or he wish for the man or woman to get bad luck at all times.

Within two weeks of discharging himself from hospital, Harry hired a couple of young friends to drive him to Coeur d'Alene, Idaho, to see an Indian doctor who he thought might be able to help him. It was a long and strenuous trip.

> We travel on that road, we musta pass 30 to 50 trucks to every mile. Im a Def but I can Heard the Hinde wheel singing a song I used to sing, Oh Mollie. Wendy, do you remember that song I sing?... I see the Indian Doctor. He works on me at Sunday night and tell me not to expect to get Better right away.... tell me to use medicine everyday for about 2 weeks or more. (Letter, September 24, 1982)

When his leg failed to respond to the Indian doctor's treatment, Harry became very discouraged. We suggested that he try a ninety-year-old Chinese herbalist we knew in Vancouver. He agreed, and so Michael and I drove to Hedley with our week-old son, Leithen, to pick him up. In Vancouver, we delivered him every other day over the course of a month to Dr. Lee and his daughter. In the middle of Harry's treatment, just as his sore showed signs of closing, Dr. Lee died. Dejected, Harry returned to his home at Hedley to treat his leg on his own. The fight against this malady—hours and hours of changing bandages and applying ointments—consumed Harry. By the fall of 1983, he was so weak that he stayed in bed almost constantly. In a short letter of September 23, he explained that "I might make it or may not. I was so weak and so low in my condition....I more like to laid down in Bed then anythink els." Again he sought an Indian doctor for help: "the Indian Doctor were here. him and his wife on the 1st day of November. that night thee work on me for two night. Left on the 3rd." (Letter, November 4, 1983)

By early spring of 1984, Harry finally asked Carrie, his neighbour, to call an ambulance. Back at the Princeton Hospital, he was close to death. After several months of intravenous feedings, he regained his strength, and eventually he recovered. At this point, he moved out of his small bungalow into the Pine Acres Home, a senior citizens' complex owned and operated by the Westbank Indian Band. Other than the hospital, this was Harry's first experience with institutionalization, and he did not like it. He missed his home, and most of all he missed his Similkameen Valley: "Im kinda lonesome. Is noone to talket with."

After a year, Harry transferred to Mountainview Manor, a seniors' complex located in Keremeos. Here he was finally happy, especially with the thorough home-care provided by his band. Harry lived for almost three years here, sleeping a lot and eating too little. He continued to tell stories, but the vigour was going.

On November 13, 1989, Michael and I travelled to Keremeos to launch *Write It on Your Heart*. It was a big day for all of us. We had circulated word about the event widely. Harry dressed for the occasion and was wheeled the several blocks to the hall, where he was enthusiastically fêted by a hundred of his people. He spoke to his friends, he sang and he drummed. He signed books carefully and precisely, one by one. After he had finished, he watched a slide presentation while the local drumming group sang in his honour. When we said good-bye the next day, it was for the last time.

"NOTHING I CAN DO BUT TELL STORIES"

Although Harry had loved listening to stories as a child, he did not become a serious storyteller until late in life.

> I forget for a long time and I never thought. But the older I get, the older I come, and it seems to come back on me. Just like I think and I could see, like. It just seems to come back. That's the way I remember. But, for a long time, I forget. I didn't remember. But when I get older and nothing I can do but tell stories. And then I begin to see 'em. And people. Remember again.

In a way, storytelling filled the gap created by the loss of ranch work. "I can go for twenty-one hours or more when I get started," he explained, "because this is my job. I'm a storyteller." In his prime, Harry had a huge repertoire that he could perform with ease in both Okanagan and English.

Harry learned many of his stories from his maternal grandmother,

Louise Newhmkin. While her daughter Arcell worked, Louise looked after Harry. But the arrangement was a reciprocal one. Because Louise was partly blind, Harry also cared for his grandmother. During their many hours together, Louise told her young grandson stories. There were others who told Harry stories, too—John Ashnola, who was in his nineties when he died in the 1918 flu epidemic, and Mary Narcisse, who was close to one hundred when she died in 1944.

Harry recalled that, as a child, he was never content to let a story go unfinished.

They tell stories anytime. And we just sometimes maybe just myself and tell me the stories. But sometimes we need two, three of us. And tell the stories for maybe a couple of hours, the old people. And they stop, because they can't talk too long, you know. They too old to keep talking, you know. They can tell the stories about a couple of hours, maybe three hours, and they have to stop. And if we remember just whereabout, and next day or anytime after we could remind 'em.

"You tell the stories that much. But you should've tell me some more about it."

"Oh yeah, I can tell you. I can tell you the rest of it anytime, you know."

Then they tell me the rest of 'em. And that's the way we do. That is how you learn, that is, if you enjoy the stories. But some of them, they don't care, you know. Whenever the old people stop telling, then they forget. They don't care. I always remember and I like to know. I want to hear the stories till they get to the end. So that is the way that happens.

The setting for most of Harry's storytelling was the front room of his bungalow. At a small Arborite table precisely laid out with his pens, papers, scissors, white-out (for correcting his letters), knives, rulers, cigarettes, ashtrays and matches, Harry felt at ease. He usually initiated a story after dinner. Except for pauses to smoke his Players cigarettes or to suck on peppermints, he spoke without interruption for several hours at a time. His only prop was a continuous series of striking hand gestures, indeed a whole hand language that told the story almost as a manual dance. Harry stopped only when he thought I was tired, usually around midnight.

FROM *WRITE IT ON YOUR HEART*
TO *NATURE POWER*

In the beginning, I listened to the stories without running my tape recorder. However, as I began to appreciate the cultural depth and historic importance of Harry's unique artistry, I saw the need to record the stories he told. According to Harry, no one had made a systematic record of them. So one day I proposed to do this. Without hesitation, he responded, "All right. Go ahead."

For neither of us was this an "extractive" exercise. Harry rejected the idea of payment, which is common in anthropological fieldwork.

> If you want to know, I'm willing to tell you stories at any time. You
> don't have to pay me. If you happened to be around I might need your
> help, or may not. Just depends. (Letter, February 7, 1981)

Harry never launched spontaneously into a story. He was always thinking ahead, and he planned his stories well in advance of my visits. Usually, sometime after dinner, he would announce, often without any explanation, "Now, I'm going to tell you number one stories. 'There was a man...'" Thus would a story begin. At the end, he would announce abruptly, "That's the end of that story. Now, here is number two stories."

I did not interrupt while the stories were in progress. He told whatever he felt like telling, and my tape recorder appeared not to bother him. Other than telling me to turn it off during a smoke break, he made little reference to the machine.

The stories Harry told me were always in English. Since an increasing number of his listeners over the years spoke only English, he decided to translate his stories to keep them alive. By the time I met him, he had become as skilled at telling his stories in English as he was in the Okanagan language.

I first proposed to Harry by letter that we turn his stories into a book. He responded with enthusiasm.

> About you going to write a Book about me. my stories. I think that is
> a good idea. Do it while Im life yet. You have saying you going to start
> it written in March. Go right ahead. Im agree about it. (Letter, February 1985)

About my stories, its on tape already for you to put that on Book. But
still you want me to Help you on some when you doing that. Oh I will
do what I can for the rest of you want to know. (Letter, March 1, 1985)

With support from the Canada Council Explorations program, we
began our work. Although he followed the project closely and partic-
ipated directly in certain components of it, such as suggesting items
to be included and collecting old family photographs, Harry en-
couraged me to take the lead in organizing the book's contents.

that's really up to you. don't have to ask me about it. I wrote the some
of it or I mention on tape and you do the rest of the work. The stories
is worked by Both of us you and I. (Letter, January 27, 1986)

And so I did, listening again to the entire tape collection and
selecting from it a representative cross section that I organized into
four sections: stories about creation and the animal-people, stories
about the early human ancestors, stories about power (the shoo-MISH)
and stories about Native-White interactions throughout the past century. These stories were published in *Write It on Your Heart*.

This second volume focusses on Harry's stories about "nature
power," the life-sustaining spirituality that guided Harry throughout
his life.

You got to have power. You got to, the kids, you know. They got to
meet the animal, you know, when they was little. Can be anytime till
it's five years old to ten years old. He's supposed to meet animal or
bird, or anything, you know. And this animal, whoever they meet,
got to talk to 'em and tell 'em what they should do. Later on, not right
away. And that is his power. And when the time comes, then they
could sing his song. Then he was an Indian doctor. Then he can do the
way he was told. Just like going to school. The little boy or little girl,
they send 'em out in nighttime, the Indians do, send 'em out. Just the
one. Just by himself. Send 'em out and tell 'em, maybe they were hunting someplace, then they come down off the hill, way down the road
somewhere. Then they could leave something near the road, maybe
leave horn, deer horn. Or maybe cut off the heart. Leave the heart
there, something for the kids to go get 'em. And bring 'em. And they
might, after supper, after dark. And tell the boy or girl, "You go over
there." And showed them whereabouts. "I left something there. You

go over and get them and bring 'em here." Well, this boy, they got to go. They got to be over there. And even if they don't like it, if they're scared, but they got to go. And when they get there, or before they get there, they might meet some animal on the way going that way, or coming back. Or maybe that's the one that they went to get, that's the one that will talk to 'em. Then, when they come back, well, they got the power already. And they wouldn't say. But whoever send 'em, they know. And that's how they get the power.

The first section of *Nature Power*, "You Got To Have Power," features five stories of initial encounters with power-helpers (shoo-MISH). Although the stories are quite different from one another, they have one thing in common. In each a child is either taken to an isolated place and left there by parents and relatives or sent at night to an isolated place to retrieve some part of an animal. While alone, each meets his or her shoo-MISH.

Although invisible, this power is very real. "They got the power in them, in their arms, in their body," Harry explained, "but you cannot see it."

If there was a fan, I could bring it and sit it here and the wheel is not turning. Then I take this wire and put 'em over there on the plug. The same second, and it'll turn. It'll turn by the power. Pull that out, and this wheel, it'll stop. Did you see that power come through the wire? No. Can't see. Indian, the same way. You can't see their power.

The second section, "Power Just for Themselves," presents five stories about the interaction between individuals and their shoo-MISH during times of crisis. Although the encounter with one's shoo-MISH occurs early in life, the power-helper does not reappear until one is in need, often much later. Many shoo-MISH offer protection to humans "just for themselves," not for others.

Or if they got the children, they can use his own power for his children, or his wife, and that's all, because they're not told by the other bird or animal, or whatever they talked to 'em, to have a power, they don't tell 'em to use their power for somebody else.

"Power To Do the Doctoring," the third section of the book, features four stories about healing others through the shoo-MISH. "Was told by the bird or animal," explained Harry. "He can do to any-body. He can use his power to anybody what was sick or get hurt, anything like that. And that's what they call the Indian doctor."

Although Harry was trained in the ways of the shoo-MISH, he never acquired his own: "I was sent out a few times, but I never see nothing." Consequently, he considered himself vulnerable to sick-ness and bad luck. "People without shoo-MISH, if they got trouble or something then what can they do? They got no power to get the trouble away from them." For this reason, Harry had to go to Indian doctors for a cure when he fell ill.

Whoever they didn't have shoo-MISH, they got to hire Indian doctor. Just like me. Because I got no shoo-MISH. But I was sick, and I know what's the matter, but I can't do it. And I got to get Indian doctor to do that for me. But if I had shoo-MISH like the other people, well, I can do it myself.

There were many Indian doctors, each of whom was responsible for curing different ailments.

See? The Indian power, the Indian doctor, the power person, they not all the same. Each one, they got a little different way in their power. They good for certain things, but they not good for the others. Maybe another Indian doctor can be good for the others, but what he know, this other one, they don't know that. See? That's the way it goes. Then, there's a lot of different ways. Some of them power person or Indian doctor, this power, they call it shoo-MISH. That's his power. That was the animal they talked to 'em. Doesn't matter what kind of animal. Any animal—bear or grizzly or wolf or coyote or deer, any animal can talk to 'em. And they can tell 'em, the same animal, they can tell 'em: "You look at that. And take a look. And you could see a man or woman. They're already in a bad way. You do this. You go and do this." Show them what to do to save 'em. To be all right. He got to be told by his power. And they can go and do that, what they was told. And they saved him or her from getting in a bad way.

Whenever he could, Harry attended the *shnay-WHUM,* the winter dances in which people sang in honour of their shoo-MISH. Not only were the sick doctored at these events, but just dancing there to support the singers was better than any insurance policy that money could buy. The story "Don't Forget My Song" describes Harry's own experience with an Indian doctor at one of these winter dances.

The stories in the fourth and final section of the book, "Encounters with Power," focus on the wide range of power experiences within the Okanagan world. In one story, "You Can't See Me, but Just Listen," a man encounters power in the form of a voice that foretells the network of highways to come. Another, "The Indians, They Got the Power," describes how some Indian doctors stopped a train with their shoo-MISH. Yet another recounts how a Hedley boy was picked up by a large gorillalike creature and transported to a community many miles away. "She Was Dead at One Time, but She Come Alive" tells the story of several people who died and returned to life.

"QUITE A BIT OF DIFFERENCE BETWEEN THE WHITE PEOPLE AND THE INDIANS"

From the beginning of our friendship, Harry was preoccupied with power, whether in the context of his own health or in relation to the history of his people. During one of our first taped sessions in 1979, he referred to the source of this power in his creation story, a story that he told many times throughout our years together, sometimes in full, sometimes in fragments. Reproduced in *Write It on Your Heart* as "Twins: White and Indian," the story explains how God, at the beginning of time, created five people, two of whom were twins. To each of the first three people he created, God gave a paper containing a set of written instructions on how to survive until the end of time. With only one paper for the two remaining brothers, God decided to go away to think about how to proceed. Before he left, however, he placed the paper under a rock and told both twins not to touch it in his absence. The younger twin became curious about the paper, and fearing that it contained something important, he disobeyed God's instruction and stole the paper without the other twin's knowledge. When God returned and asked about the missing paper, the younger twin denied knowing anything of it.

According to Harry, this younger twin, "now today, that's the White man. . . . And that's why the White man can tell a lie more than the Indian." Angered by the younger twin's action, God gave him the paper and told him that this would become the source of his power until the end of time.

> "That paper... it's going to show you how
>   you going to make it to get back here.
> But not right away.
> Long time from now....
> But when you come back, a long time from now,
>   you going to have a heck of a time.
> You're going to lose a lot of people.
> There's a lot of people
>   that's going to be drowned on that water....
> But that paper, it will show you how you going to do it.
>   to get back here."

"And the older twin," explained Harry, "that's me. That's the Indian." Instead of power in the form of paper, God gave the older twin an intangible spiritual power. "So that's why," explained Harry, "the Indian, they got a different way."

> You know, the Indians, God put the Indians in the head, you know, in the heart, for the things to know. But the White people, they got the paper. [If] they don't read the paper, they forget things. It's just like that, you know.... The Indians, just like the way I see it, because we supposed to have it on our brains, our heart, you know, the things we will remember.... Most of the Indian people know that. Because there's a lot of these White people, they don't seems to know that we are, us Indian, we are that way. They think that we don't know anything. That's what the most of 'em thinks. They thinks the Indians, they don't know nothing till the White people come. And then the White people told 'em. Then they know. But the way I tell you last night, the Indians know that from God, long long time ago before Christ.

Harry told his nature power stories to set straight the historical record so that everyone, Native and non-Native alike, would know why Whites and Indians are different. He was concerned that the deep knowledge of the past was disappearing. To illustrate this he told a story of a meeting in 1881 between the Indians and a government man in Penticton. During this meeting, the government man asked the Indians to tell him about their beginnings.

It means how come to be an Indian here in the first before the White? That's what it meant. But the Indians at that time, they doesn't know anything about it. And they try to say, but they say something different. And the other one get up and try to say something different.... They didn't know.... And one of them, he says,

"Yeah, our forefather, how we become to be
    Indian, that's from Adam, Adam and Eve."

"No, no, that's mine."

"Yeah," the one 'em says,
"Noah, Noah, the one that built that great big...
    when the world flood."

"No," he says.
"That's overseas.
    That's my forefather. Not the Indians.
    I'm asking you for your forefather."

But they don't know.... Still, they don't even know today.... Not the people know, but I do, I know.... I know how come for the Indians to be here.

Harry also believed his stories would help people, both Native and White, to understand where they came from and why their interactions have been so antagonistic. He considered these to be important stories that should be circulated widely: "Is not to be Hidden," he wrote. "It is to be showed in all Province in Canada and United States. that is when it comes to be a Book." (Letter, January 27, 1986)

OTHER VOICES ON NATURE POWER

Harry's accounts of Okanagan nature power are not the first to be published. During the summer of 1930, Walter Cline, a Harvard graduate student in anthropology, interviewed a number of Okanagans living on the Colville Reservation in Washington State about their religious worldview. He published his findings eight years later in a chapter of *The Sinkaietk or Southern Okanagon of Washington*, edited by Leslie Spier. (In the American spelling of "Okanagan," the third "a" is replaced by an "o.") Entitled "Religion and Worldview," this chapter, though mainly in the voice of Cline, is rich in detail. It depicts a spiritual worldview intricately linked with nature.

> The religion of the Okanagon expressed itself in the affiliation of the individual man or woman with a material object or class of objects, usually with an animal, bird, or insect. Their word sumix refers to this relationship, as well as to anything which functioned for a person in this way, and to the physical and spiritual potency which one possessed by virtue of this affiliation. When speaking English, the Okanagon translate sumix as "power" for each and all of the different meanings of sumix. . . .
>
> The Okanagon believed, in a vague way, that it resided inside him, perhaps in his chest or in his heart. When it manifested itself in his power-song, his whole body shook. One's guardian spirit dwelt somewhere in the woods or the mountains, and came to him when he thought of it or needed its aid. (p. 133)

A more vivid account comes from Okanagan writer Christine Quintasket. Before she died in 1936 at the age of forty-nine, Quintasket wrote her autobiography. Anthropologist Jay Miller edited the work, and it was published as *Mourning Dove*, Quintasket's pen name. In this, she includes a chapter entitled "Spiritual Training" that describes how Okanagan parents and grandparents trained their young. "Indian theory," she writes, "holds that each spirit has the same strengths as its animal counterpart." Quintasket's spiritual mentor was an old woman named Teequalt. Teequalt taught Christine many things, and like the spiritual mentors in Harry's stories, she led Christine along her own spiritual path:

> "If you are not afraid tonight, you will see a vision of this power I earned when I was a little girl like you. It is the power of Eagle, chief of birds."

"THE STORIES IS WORKED BY BOTH OF US, YOU AND I"

As Harry pointed out, each of us had a particular role to play in bringing his stories to a larger audience. His job was to tell stories, and mine was to get them onto the printed page. As I immersed myself in transcribing Harry's stories for *Write It on Your Heart*, however, I became more and more dissatisfied with how most oral stories are rendered. Passing through a maze of translators and editors, most stories are cut down and compulsively "cleaned up"—and thereby stripped of their drama and performance, their immediacy and their authenticity of voice. I decided to proceed differently. Because Harry had translated his own stories to perform them in English, editing was unnecessary. Here was an opportunity for readers to experience storytelling straight from the source.

In trying to remain as true to Harry's originals as possible, I did encounter some problems. The first was that Harry's words, when presented as narrative prose, were cryptic, and the stories lost the dramatic quality of their original telling. To remedy this, I decided to place them on the page in the form of narrative poetry, which brings out the unique features of Harry's style—the frequent repetition, the pauses, the sentence structure. Another problem I faced was that Harry used the pronouns "he," "she" and "they" interchangeably, which I thought would make it difficult for readers to follow the story line, particularly in places where both male and female characters were present. So I changed pronouns to modify their antecedents. And finally, because Harry's system of identifying stories either by number ("this is number three stories") or by characteristic words or phrases ("this is cat with boots on stories") would not draw the reader in, I also gave each story a title and a short, descriptive lead-in.

In preparing *Nature Power*, I have changed my editorial procedure slightly. For this book, I had two assistants helping with transcription: Blanca Chester, a graduate student in comparative literature, and Lynne Jorgesen, a Native journalist. Based on their suggestions, I have edited original pronouns only when absolutely necessary, such as in places where they clearly disrupted the flow of the story. In addition, the title for each story collected here comes from a phrase or sentence distilled from the story itself. In these ways, the stories in

Nature Power are even closer to Harry's original tellings.

Harry often used Okanagan words when telling his stories in English, mainly personal names, place names and a few well-known terms for which he preferred his first language. There is an international phonetic system for transcribing such words, but without some preliminary study of this system, words rendered in it are quite incomprehensible. In order to encourage readers to "say" the words aloud as they read the stories, I have transcribed Okanagan words roughly according to how they sound. These are crude approximations only. A list of phonetic transcriptions appears on page ___.

Different versions of two of the stories published in *Write It on Your Heart* also appear in this book—"Go Get Susan, See What She Can Do" (a retelling of "Indian Doctor") and "Power Man, Power Woman, They Each Have a Different Way" (a retelling of "A Woman Receives Power from the Deer"). I have included them here both because they are important stories on the theme of nature power and because they illustrate how Harry approached a story freshly each time he told it.

"IS NOT TO BE HIDDEN"

When *Write It on Your Heart* was released in the fall of 1989, the term "cultural appropriation" was virtually unheard of on the Canadian literary scene. I first came across it in a *Globe and Mail* op-ed piece that I happened to read while travelling to Harry's funeral in January of 1990. Entitled "Stop Stealing Native Stories," the article, by Ojibway poet and storyteller Lenore Keeshig-Tobias, attacked the Canadian cultural industry, in particular the film industry, for its marginalization of Native voices. She called it "cultural theft, the theft of voice." Having just completed *Write It on Your Heart*, I was naturally interested in her ideas.

Two years later, discussions about appropriation occupy front and centre stage, not just among First Nations peoples but in the whole literary community. Just recently, artists from across Canada attacked Joyce Zemans, director of the Canada Council, for comments she made about the council's approach to the issues of "appropriate" voice and subject matter. Within the academic community, from anthropology to historical geography, "appropriation" and "representation of voice" are key components of a growing "postmodernist critical theory." Stimulated by James Clifford and George Marcus in *Writing Culture* and George Marcus and Michael Fischer in *Anthropology as Cultural Critique*, many academics are questioning the very legitimacy of the traditional "scientific" approach to the study of the cultural "other," that is, the very *process* of objective research. British-based literary theorist David Murray, in his recent book *Forked Tongues*, argues that most North American texts are "representations" permeated with ideology, much of which can be related to the power relations embedded in the dominant society.

Today the Native community continues to drive this critical awareness. Where anthropologists talk about false representation, Native commentators decry the appropriation of their voices. At a forum entitled "Telling Our Own Story," held in Vancouver in January 1990, members of the Committee to Re-establish the Trickster criticized the "silencing of the real Native voices that do exist right now and have existed for thousands of years." They asserted that Native peoples have a right to be heard.

Nature Power attempts to be respectful of these concerns. Harry Robinson wanted his stories to be heard, because he knew they contained important knowledge. As the artifice of the White world enveloped everything around him, Harry wanted *everyone*—Native and non-Native—to understand that there were ways other than those of the White man. He was haunted by the possibility that his knowledge would die with him: "I'm going to disappear, and there'll be no more telling stories."

My role has been to help Harry reach a broader audience with his stories. But I am also present as listener and collaborator. I cannot speak for Harry or for the Okanagan people, but I can speak from what I have learned. I was close to Harry; I travelled with him and cared for him. My world and my way of thinking were changed by this experience. Harry knew this. When he was gravely ill in the spring of 1983, he spoke to Michael and me in perhaps the most serious tone I had ever heard him use. He told us,

> So, take a listen to these, a few times and think about it, to these stories, and what I tell you now. Compare them. See if you can see something more about it. Kind of plain, but it's pretty hard to tell you for you to know right now. Takes time. And then you will see. And him [Michael]. That's all. No more stories. Do you understand?

These words have remained with me.

One thing I learned from Harry was that he never fictionalized stories. Indeed, the very concept of fiction was foreign to him. This was driven home to me about a year ago while I was spinning through a reel of Department of Indian Affairs documents reproduced on microfilm. As I passed by file after file, I suddenly recognized something—the 1889 letters from the relatives of "Ashnola George" (written in the hand of an Oblate priest, Father LeJeune) directed to the warden of the British Columbia Penitentiary in New Westminster. The letters revealed a desperate search by an Okanagan woman for the body of her nephew, whom she was told had died at the prison.

I had heard Harry tell that story and had reproduced it in *Write It on Your Heart* as "Captive in an English Circus." The archival account backed up Harry's version on every point, even though Harry had been told the story twenty years after it had taken place—and had recounted it to me a full century later! Moreover, unlike the formal records, Harry's account reveals what actually happened to George Jim, who had been abducted from the prison and taken to England where he spent his life as a circus showpiece.

The stories in *Nature Power* are also true. Yet many of them deal with things that on one level seem fantastic—people dying and then returning to life, people materializing from natural objects, disembodied voices predicting the future, and so on. Are we to take such stories seriously? Having spent time with Harry Robinson, having experienced his precision and clarity and knowledge, I certainly do. Indeed, the truth and accuracy of Harry's words in *Nature Power* have made me think anew about what is "real," what we "know," what is "true." In the West we have built a civilization around the "true" story of a man who died and was resurrected after three days. The people in Harry's stories experienced nature deeply and directly in a way that I cannot know, but that Harry wanted me, and others, to appreciate. To Harry, great powers in life were to be gained from encounters with natural beings, from relationships with nature and with the land. Perhaps not all of us can "know" the truth of this world, but hearing from one who does should change our consciousness.

Today the future of the planet is at stake. Everywhere traditional cultures are dying, and nature is dying with them. As Chief John Tetlenitsa of Spence's Bridge, a community not far from Hedley, explained as early as 1912, "The *snams* [the Nlaka'pamux equivalent of the Okanagan shoo-MISH] are forgetting us nowadays because of the coming of the white man. They are leaving the country." Harry Robinson's stories convey a very different cultural understanding of, and relationship to, nature. They explain the long-standing antagonism between Native peoples and White people, and its source in that simple White lie told at the beginning of time. From this lie, two forms of power emerged—one, the "power of nature," and the other, the "power of paper and writing." As the presence of old people like Harry recedes into historical distance, more and more people—academic and non-academic, Native and non-Native—question whether the world that Harry depicts was ever "real," whether it ever existed. Drawing on both traditions of power, *Nature Power* provides an answer.

At the launch in Keremeos, after years of waiting patiently (one of Harry's home-care assistants believed that in the final months of his life the wait for the book had kept him alive), Harry finally witnessed the ceremonial blessing of his book by the Okanagan spiritual leader Napoleon Kruger. Harry will not be able to launch *Nature Power* himself, but I hope that readers will follow his instructions.

> Take a listen to these
>   a few times
>   and think about it. . . .
> See if you can see something more. . . .
> Takes time, and then you will see.

REFERENCES

Barbeau, Marius. "How the Twin Sisters' Song Saved Tetlenitsa," *The Star Weekly Magazine,* 10 January 1959.

Clifford, James, and George Marcus. *Writing Culture: The Poetics and Politics of Ethnography.* Berkeley: University of California Press, 1986.

Cline, Walter. "Religion and Worldview." In *The Sinkaietk or Southern Okanagon of Washington,* edited by Leslie Spier. General Series in Anthropology, No. 6. Menasha: George Banta Publishing Co., 1938.

"Frightening Attack on the Imagination," *The Globe and Mail*, 28 March 1992. Letters to the editor.

Godfrey, Stephen. "Canada Council Asks Whose Voice Is It Anyway?" *The Globe and Mail*, 21 March 1992.

Keeshig-Tobias, Lenore. "Stop Stealing Native Stories," *The Globe and Mail*, 26 January 1990.

Marcus, George E., and Michael J. Fischer. *Anthropology as Cultural Critique: An Experimental Movement in the Social Sciences.* Chicago: University of Chicago Press, 1986.

Mourning Dove. *Mourning Dove: A Salishan Autobiography.* Edited by Jay Miller. Lincoln, Nebraska: University of Nebraska Press, 1990.

Murray, David. *Forked Tongues: Speech, Writing and Representation in North American Indian Texts.* Bloomington: Indiana University Press, 1991.

"Telling Our Own Story: Appropriation and Indigenous Writers and Performing Artists." Vancouver: January 1990. Report.

PART I

YOU GOT TO
HAVE POWER

YOU THINK IT'S
A STUMP, BUT THAT'S
MY GRANDFATHER

Left alone by his father, his uncles and the other hunters, a boy finds himself singing with another young boy and his grandfather beside a smooth stump.

Shash-AP-kin.
That's his Indian name.
White people call it Shash-AP-kin.
Indians call it Shash-ap-KANE.
That means "Smooth Stump."
Supposing if—now here's this—
    that's the stump right there.
And underneath the stump was washed out
    and washed out,
        and then there's kind of hole underneath.
The roots look like that.
And it's kind of—the chipmunk or anything can get under
    that.
And this stump was a-standing in the place
    where this snow slide at every year.
But, they must've grow there a long, long time.
But maybe not sliding place at that time.
But somehow, when the earthquake and the rocks was sliding,
    and they open up like—
        and when the snow comes
            and after that slide every year.

But this tree was growing there right where the slide goes.
But hit by a big stone and broke.
But only stump—so high.

The stump is still there.
It turn into a hard wood, more like a pitch.
Then every time when they had a snow slide,
  it was always mixed with rocks and things, you know.
Then the rocks, the small rocks, they hit them
  and—just like they resting or something.
And they smooth.
Just smooth, but stump.
And underneath, they kind of washed.
And there was kind of hole underneath.

But right in the steep hill
  and the place was like that.
That's where the snow slide every year.
And Shash-AP-kin, he was just a young,
  about ten years old, eleven years old,
      something like that.
And he was left there by the hunter.
His dad, and the other hunters, they tell 'em,

    "You stay here.
      You wait here.
      It's too far for you to walk.
      You stay 'round here.
      We can hunt that way, make a turn
        and a circle,
          and then we come back.
      Towards evening we come by
        and then you can go back with us to the camp."

You know, they tell 'em lies to leave 'em there.
Just like George Jim.
Yeah.
So the older people, his dad and his uncle and the others,
  they thought they going to leave him there by himself.

Maybe some animal, maybe bird or something,
   they might met them.
And talk to 'em.
So he can be power man.
They think—but they didn't tell 'em.
They just tell 'em,

> "You, you might get tired if you go along.
>   You too young.
>   You going to get tired.
>   You stay here and we hunt.
>   We come back and then you can go back with us
>   to the camp."

So he thinks,

> "Well, that's good enough,
>   because that's too far.
>   I get tired if I go along."

So he satisfied to be there alone.
So these other people went.
But he's left there all by himself.
So finally, he looked around and he go down that way
   where he could see that the nice and smooth.
Quite a ways.
Where the snow slide.
But this was in the summer—no snow.
So he looked that place
   and then he could see that stump,
      quite a ways down.
So he thought,

> "Maybe I go and see that.
>   Looks like a rock or looks like a stump or something.
>   Maybe I go down there and take a look."

So he went down and he come to this stump.
Before he get too close,

and he looked.
By God, that stump was just as smooth,
  just like somebody rub it nice and smooth.
And they go little ways.
Looked around.
Then they see the chipmunk.
Running from little ways.
And they run to get under that stump.
Because it's high from the ground
  and they get under that.

He pick up a stick,
  and he thought he go over there
    and is going to make a fun with that chipmunk.
He put the stick underneath, you know.
He going to scare 'em out of there
  and then he's going to make 'em run away.
Or else, he's going to make fun.

When he get there,
  and he get the stick,
    and they puts the stick under the stump, you know,
      to try to get the chipmunk out of that.
But, the first thing they do,
  the chipmunk, it get out of that stump on the other side.
But he get up.
And there was another boy, like him.
Just a boy, just like him.
Get out of the stump and he stand up.
Was another boy.
And told 'em,

    "Well, boy, you're here."

    "Yeah."

    "You think you're going to make a fun out of me."

    "Well," he says.
    "That's what I think."

"You do not think of that.
   You my friend.
   You boy, and I'm a boy.
   We both boy.
   So, it's better to be friends
      instead of making fun out of me.
   Now, I'm going to tell you something.
   This stump—you think it's a stump—
      but that's my grandfather.
   He's very, very old man.
   Old, old man.
   He can talk to you.
   He can tell you what you going to be.
   When you get to be middle-aged, or more.
   But you're not going to be like that now,
      right away.
   Later on.
   When you get to be middle-aged.
   My grandfather that will tell you . . ."

Then, just in a second, then he could see,
   supposed to be the son
   but he was an old, old man.
He setting there.
And he talked.
And told 'em,

   "You see me.
      You see my body.
      It was hit by the bullet for many, many years.
      Hit by the bullet.
      That's why you could see, all smooth.
      That's bullet marks.
      And the bullet, when they hit me—the bullet—
         they never go through my skin.
      They never go through my body.
      For a long, long time.
      You look how old I was.
      I been hit with a bullet for many years.
      I never get killed.

The bullet never go in through my body.
So now, that's the way you going to be.
When you get to be a man.
If somebody shoots you,
       with the bow and arrow, or gun."

At those days, they had the gun,
   like the first gun like they have.

"Then, if anybody shoot you,
       you going to be just like me.
   The bullet never will go into your skin.
   And that's going to be your power."

And he started to sing.
He sing the song.
That old man.
And the chipmunk was a boy,
   turn to be a boy.
He sing the song.
The both of 'em talked to him.
And he's got two power.
And he sing the song.
The three of 'em sing the song,
   for a while.
Then told 'em that, that would be enough.
Then, in the same way, he don't know what happened
   and he went to sleep.

First thing he know, he was WAY down.
He must've rolled, or sliding, or somehow,
       but WAY down.
When he wake up.
And he wake up and then his people were around,
   way up there, looking for him.
They couldn't find 'em.
But he get up and he could see his people WAY up.
And then he got up and they holler.
Then, these other people,

My God!, they holler way down.
They must've go down that way.

But the last he knew, right by that stump.
No more.
But he might've walked down or might've rolled.
Nobody know.
But he was WAY down when they come to him.

But he knows already what he's going to be
    when he get to be a man.
So, that's the way he get his power.
Then, when he get to be a man,
    'bout middle age or more,
        and told him again,

        "Now is his time. For you.
            You're not going to use your power for anybody.
            Just for you."

So that's Shash-AP-kin is a power man
    but his power, never use for anybody,
        you know, just for himself.

Then, one time, just so they could show, I think,
    somehow that they had trouble with the white people.
And finally these white people,
    those days, all the white people that comes,
        they all bad, you know.
They mean.
They tough.
So they—they shoot him.
He shoot him with a rifle.
But they never get him.
They never kill him.
Those days, there's different rifles they use.
They got the powder they put right in the rifle.
Then put the lead in there
    and put the rag in there

and put powder to the rag.
Then put some more rags.
Then they put the lead in.
And then they put some more rags on top of the lead,
   to keep the lead in place.
Then—they got the hammer just like the other gun.
Then they pull the trigger.
Then this is expired or exploded.
Then the bullet went, "Bang!"
Then they smoke.
They fired two shots.
They got two bar, you know, more like a shotgun.
Fire the both of 'em.
Quite the smoke.

When they shoots him with that.
When the smoke was all over,
   he still there.
He never gots hurt.
The bullet never go in.
But they know, they shoot him not far.
They hit it all right.
But the bullet never go through on his body.
And that's just to show to the white,
   or to the other Indians.
So that's how they know he's a power man.
Just for himself.
So he live till he get old.
Very old—can be about seventy or more.

POWER MAN,
POWER WOMAN,
THEY EACH HAVE
A DIFFERENT WAY

A young girl is instructed by her father to go and fetch the heart of a deer.
As she approaches the designated place, she hears someone singing a song.

[There] was a girl, way big enough to walk for three, four
    miles.
Must've been ten years old.
Maybe eleven or maybe twelve.
And they were up on the mountain,
    her and her folks, you know.
And some other people.
Two, three camps on the mountain.
Not too high—that's in the fall.
And they put in the camp and the mans . . . go . . . hunting.
And when they get deer,
    then they bring them.
And the ladies, that was their job, to cut the meat,
    you know.
Cut it and dry 'em.
Dry 'em on the smoke.
They make a place to dry the meat, you know.
They fix up and tie the sticks together like that,
    and then one across here.
Then they put some pole right on top there.
Then they lie the grass

so they can put the meat on top of that.
And there's a lot of air and the smoke can come, you know.
They make a small fire,
    use only certain kind of wood.
They make a fire underneath and then that burns,
    but mostly smoke.
And the meat can get dry that way in a couple days
    or they can keep 'em there maybe two night.
Two days and the meat will be dry.
The women do that.
That's their job.

But the mans, they go out and hunt
    and get a deer and bring 'em.
In other way, they can roast 'em on a stick, you know,
    on the open fire.
And cook them that way.
And it can be keep, you know.
Keep them for the winter.

And bunch of them, they have the camp,
    maybe three, four camps.
And her dad were out on mountain, hunting,
    and he got a deer.
And he drag the deer from the mountainside and downhill
    towards the trail.
And there was a creek and here is that.
And here is the sketch for that.
This would be the creek, see.
And they drag the deer from—
    like from this side—towards the trail.
And here is the trail—this little line.
And here is the camp.
And this is the trail—could be about two, three miles.
And—yeah—could be three miles, this trail.
From the camp to the creek.

And they kill the deer up on hillside
    and then they drag 'em this way
        towards the trail and to the creek.

And the trail goes across the creek.
And they drag the deer from there to here.
Then they leave 'em there,
 near the trail, and near the creek.

And then they cut 'em open.
Then they clean out and they cut the heart.
Off.
And, after they cut the heart off,
 then they clean 'em
  and they put the heart inside of it, you know.
In the ribs, like, inside of it.
And then they put—
 break some boughs, branches, you know,
  and put it on the ground.
That's where they cut 'em open and clean 'em.
And then lay them that way and broke some more
 and then they cover 'em.
With the branches, you know.
They put branches over 'em—clean around.

But the heart, they put it inside of it.
And they took the trail and go to camp.
And they get to the camp,
 and it's kind of late—getting to be dark.
And they have supper and after that it would be around eight
 o'clock.
Or a little more.
And he tell the girl, that was his daughter, tell her—
He says to her,

 "I want you to go on this trail with that creek
  where the trail goes across the creek.
  And I left the deer on the other side of the trail.
  Near the creek."

She know that.
She been through there before.
He told 'em whereabout.
Told 'em,

"You go over there.
  Tonight.
  And I cut the heart off for you.
  Cut 'em off and I put 'em in there just for a while.
  And I put 'em in and I go down the creek
    and wash my hands and come back
      and I was going to bring that heart.
  And I forget."

And that's his excuse, you know.
Just so she can get there.
See, he leave that—he mean it.
But that's what he tell her daughter—his daughter.
Said,

"You bring that heart.
  Tonight.
  Doesn't matter what time you come back.
  Midnight, or towards morning.
  Don't go too fast.
  Take your time.
  But when you get near to that deer,
    that one I killed which lay there,
      you might hear something.
  You might hear a noise.
  Maybe sounds like somebody was singing.
  If you hear that kind of a sound.
  Don't run away.
  Don't come back.
  Keep going.
  And keep going that way.
  Maybe, just before you get to that deer,
    you might see something.
  And keep going.
  Don't turn back.
  Till you get close.
  And then you will see something
    and maybe someone, they might tell you something.
  And be sure to know what it was.
  And then go there and bring that heart.

Then you come back.
If you wanted, you can sleep on the way coming back.
Now, you can get here when it's daylight.
That is, if you want.
Or else you can keep coming and get back anytime."

All right.
This girl, she started.
On that trail—it's quite a ways—about, oh, a mile.
Was told not to go fast.
Take a lot of time.
When she get near to that deer,
   she know where it was.
And she know she get near.
And she could hear—sounds like the wind blowing or
   something like that.
Sounds like coyote howling or something.
Stand for a while, and listen.
Was told not to turn 'round, not to go back.
To keep going.
The closer she gets to that deer
   and the louder they could hear that,
      they knowed it was a song.
Somebody sing a song.

They keep going.
Till she get close.
She can see that deer.
It lay there—the dead one.
And then she see another one
   standing alongside of dead there.
And this one, it was alive—standing.
And they keep going and they get there.
And that one, it was alive,
   the one that standing alongside the dead one,
      he is the one that sing the song.
And till they get close and told 'em,

    "Well, little girl, you got to—
       you get here just in time.

I didn't quite finish my song, singing.
When I finish that, then away I go.
And you'll be too late.
But, you get here in time.
That was good.
You see that boy, that deer lay there?"

She said,

"Yeah. I seen 'em."

And told 'em,

"That was my body.
That's my body.
Here.
But this one here, that was my soul.
But, I can turn around and go.
And, before morning, and they just like that one that
dead.
The same one, but this one here's dead.
But, that was me and I go.
And I come alive.
Then, when you get old,
when you get the few grey on your hair,
just a few, not too much, maybe five or six in your
hair, grey—turn go white.
That would be the time to get back on you.
I'll get back on you.
Then, you can do nothing to anybody,
but for yourself.
If you get sick—if you got really sick—
you can send someone—
maybe your daughter, maybe your son, maybe your
husband, maybe your brother, ANYBODY.
Send 'em out on the mountain
and they broke some branches off the spruce.
Spruce branches.
They could broke them and tie 'em
and pack 'em on his back or pack 'em on a horse.

And get back to where you was.
You sick, that is if you sick.
Then, if you're too sick to do it,
  get someone to put 'em on the ground and in the tepee
    or house, whatever it is.
And the bed that you're on,
  take 'em away—not that one . . .
Put these branches for your bed.
Nothing but branches.
Then, might cover 'em with a light blanket.
Just one.
And then you lay there.
And you can be covered with one light blanket.
And someone can put these branches on top of your
  blanket.
On top of you.
All over—from your feet up to here.
Then you lay there.
Till morning.
Then you lay that way all day.
Two night, and one day.
Then you can take that branches away,
  and it's all right.
No more sick.
That's you only.
You can do that for yourself, protect yourself.
You fix up yourself—you get better.
When sometimes—anytime—you might get sick,
  you do that.
Or if you get hurt, you might broken leg
  or something like that.
You get hurt—same way.
If you get hurt, you use the branches.
You put 'em on the ground and lay there.
No pillow.
You can make the branches higher just for your head—
  to be higher.
Then cover them with the other one.
For one, two night and one day."

So, long time after that, when they gets kind of old,
    and one time they was sick.
They was very sick.
And, that's in Westbank.
And they got some neighbour.
Their neighbour lived there, about a mile from her place.
Some of them.
And some of them not too far.
And this, her friend, is still living yet.
Their name Eli.
Aleck Eli and his wife.
And there was a rodeo in Omak.
And they wanted to go over there,
    this Aleck and his wife.
But their neighbour was sick, they know that.
Some people told 'em they very sick.
They might die.
But, they wanted to go to the rodeo.
So, Aleck and his wife, they figured that out.
They thought, well,

    "We better go and see the old lady.
        We go to the rodeo anyway.
        We better go and see 'em.
        While we're over there, she might be die.
        Mighta' be they dead.
        Go see 'em, and we could see 'em
            when they're alive."

So they thought that after they see 'em
    and then they go.
So they went over there.
Get to the house and that lady, they got the son.
And the son got a wife and they got a family.
They lived there together.
And her son was outside, you know.
Outside the house.
They must've been chopping, something like that.
They working.

And they come to 'em and they ask him.
They says,

> "We come to see the old lady.
>   How is she?"

And the man told 'em,

> "Well, it's very sick but I think things is all right.
>   You can go in and see."

He told 'em,

> "Because we want to see 'em
>   and then we want to go to the rodeo."

Says,

> "All right.
>   You go in and see 'em."

And they turn 'round, towards the house to go in there.
Then tell 'em,

> "Wait a minute."

Then they stop.
And told 'em,

> "Don't you get surprised.
>   Don't you get excited when you go in.
>   You might see her in different way at her bed.
>   And don't mind that.
>   That's her way.
>   Just see 'em and talk to 'em.
>   And you might see something different you never see
>   before.
>   Don't get surprised or kind of excited.
>   That's her way.
>   I must let you know that before you seen 'em."

All right.
They go in.
As soon as they go in, then they see the old lady
   who laying there covered with the branches all over—
      up to here.
And no bed, no blankets, just the branches.
And they lay there.
And then they was covered with the branches all over.
And nobody see that.
That's a new way, like.
That's her way.
Nobody else but her.
Because, her dad, when he kill the deer
   and they left 'em there—
      drag 'em and they leave 'em.
Then they go out and they broke some branches,
   bunch of them and then they bring them
      and they put them on the ground.
And then they drag the deer and put them on the branches.
Then they cut 'em open and clean 'em
   and when they finished with them,
      they lay them better if it's kind of froze,
         getting stiff and then they can be all right.
Be easier to pick 'em up.
Then they get some more branches
   and then cover 'em with that.
That's why she do that.
That is why.
And the medicine at the same time.

Then they were there for another one day,
   one night.
So, for two night and one day.
She get all right.
She get better.
That's her power.
That's the way get her power.
That's one way they get the power.

All the Indian doctor, or power man, or power woman,
　each one they had a different way to get their power.
Not the same.
Each one, they got a little different way.
So that's one way, one person they get,
　they protect herself that way,
　　maybe once or twice in her life.
That's all.
That was her power.
So, that's that.
That's all.

I was looking for one more.
And she lived till she get very old.
She lived, some people says.
She was supposed to be eighty-three years old when she died.
She got sick and died.
But, you know, they live long time.
So that's the end of that story.

R A I N B O W   A T   N I G H T

A young girl follows her father's instructions and finds herself receiving an important message from an animal.

Now this is part of the power person
  how do they get their power in the first place
    that's one of 'em.
I did tell you the others but different ways
  and this is different.
But the same, they get their power
  at the first time
    but they got different way.

And I make a sketch here.
And all this, this is the mountain.
That's mountain, they got a point.
And this is another mountain,
  and this is another mountain,
    right around here.
This line from the top of the mountain,
  right from the point
    and it went down to this one.
And that's a rainbow.
That's a rainbow.
And this is the dead cow, lays right there.
The dead cow.
And this child, just a young girl
  can be about twelve years old, maybe ten years old
    heard that they got some cattle—lots of cattle . . .
And they sell the cattle and the old cow.

They know they old cow.
The cow, whenever it get old and
  some years they didn't have calf.
As long as they didn't have calf, why they get fat.
They're real fat.
Then they could sell them.
But some of the cows,
    the cows, even when they got no calves and they get fat
      still they don't sell them.
They keep 'em.
And there was three or four, sometimes.
But the other one, they died quite a while,
  and three more.
Now they all died but only the one.
When that died, they got to send out,
  they got to send out four more after that.
But they still only one more.
And they old, very old
  and in winter—well, not in winter,
    when it get to be springtime,
      like maybe in March, something like that,
        they still have them in—still feeding them.
And they always watch every day when they feed the cows
  and watch for that old cow.
And one day, one morning, they feed the cattle
  and they miss the old cow.
They not there.
So he thought maybe the old cow,
  they might die someplace.
Even if they don't die, but they might lay there
  they couldn't get up.
You know, they can lay there till they die.
So they look around for it
  after a while
    and they look.
They not far
  and they found 'em right in the field,
    right in the open.
They dead.
And that was the one right here

that was right in open—that's across the river,
   about two, three miles, two miles from here.
But on that side.
And they know that cow was dead.
And that night,
  after supper, about this time,
    could be around nine clock
      and he tell his daughter, that young girl
        he tell her
          he says to her,

"I want you to go.
  Not far from the house, about a mile.
  I want you to go to that dead cow.
  You take the knife—"
    Like the pocket knife I got, you know,
      they have that.
    He give her that.
    "—you take this knife and you go and get to that cow.
  And when you get to the cow and cut
    cut, cut her ears in the end.
  Cut 'em.
  And cut a little piece,
    put it in your pocket and bring 'em.
  So I can see.
  Whenever you come back,
    you can go over there,
      and don't go too fast.
  You go slow.
  When you get near to that cow,
    maybe two, three hundred yards before you get there,
    you might hear something.
  Might be noise.
  Might be somebody sing.
  Might be something.
  You might see something.
  And don't come back.
  And don't run away.
  Don't get scared.

Keep going.
Even if you see something,
   or hear something,
      keep going.
Don't stop
   and don't come back.
And you get to the cow,
   and cut her ear in the end
      and put it in your pocket and come back.
You might sleep on the way coming back.
Or may not.
But come back anyway, but you got to cut that off,
   and bring it so I could see that in the morning."

So that could be her proof
   that she get to that cow.
In otherwise, you know, she might go little ways
   and stop,
      and she don't go.
But if she can only cut the ear,
   the end of the ear of that cow
      well, that means she get there.
So that's the way you know
   the old man can tell that she get there.
In otherwise, you wouldn't know—
   she might get there, she may not.
All right.
Then he tell that to, tell his daughter,

   "You go.
      And if you hear something
         or see something,
            don't, don't run away.
      Keep going.
      And come back.
      You might sleep on the way coming back.
      And that don't matter.
      Whenever you wake up, if you do sleep
         you come home."

So this girl, she come.
She get near to this dead cow,
   could be around two hundred yards,
      then she get there.
Then she hear sound.
Sounds like
   wind blowing,
      or something like that,
         but she kept a-going.
Walk slow.
He told her not to go fast,
   take your time.
She be walking
   and the closer she gets
      and the louder it comes.
Finally she find out it was somebody sing a song.
There, where that cow is.
Then she kept walking and she get closer.
It was somebody singing a song.
Kinda nice,
   good song.
And she kept walking,
   and just before she get to the cow—
      maybe like from here to that wall—
         but she's got to cut that ear.
Then somehow she kinda stopped
   for a second or two.
Then she could see the . . .
   just like the lightning.
You know, when the thunder is going to come.
Before you hear the thunder,
   but you see the lightning first.
They go fast,
   just in one second.
Something like that what she seen.
She could see that from the top of the mountain.
Looks like a lightning—right down to that cow.
And in little while,
   another two, three minutes,
      two, three seconds

    then she see the other one from the other
      mountain.
She seen this one first
  from the east.
Then when it hits that cow,
  in a little while,
    just two, three seconds
      then she see the other one
        from the other mountain.
This is a creek.
Then she see the same thing to that cow.
Then in another two-three seconds
  then she seen another one from the west
    of the point of this mountain.
It went the same way,
  then they get, there was three lines.
And that was a rainbow.
But you can never see a rainbow at night.
You can see the rainbow in daytime, after the rain.
But this time it was the nighttime.
It's not raining.
But she seen a rainbow.
And she wasn't too far from that cow
  now they still there,
    and the song was still going.
And then she finished the rest of her walk,
  and then she get to the cow.
And she could see
  the rainbow right to the cow.
And her dad had told 'em
  what to say when she get close.
Supposed to talk to that cow.

    "You supposed to tell 'em,
      'I get here,
        I going to cut your ear,
          the little part of your ear, I'm going to cut it off,
            and I'm going to take it home.
        In another way, I want you to help me,
          and I want you to tell me what I should do

when I grow up.'
That's what you'll tell 'em when you get there,"
her father told her.

And she did.
When she get there,
    she could see the rainbow
        right to the cow.
But anyway, she get close, and talk to the cow,
    and went and cut that ear,
        put it in her pockets and also the knife,
            and she's going to turn round to go home.
And then they talk to 'em.
She think the cow was talking to 'em,
    the one that's dead.
And told 'em,

    "Good thing you come.
        I will tell you what you going to be from now on.
        But not right away.
        I will let you know,
            when you get about middle age.
        And then I can remind you.
        And then you going to be a power,
            power woman.
        And nothing can bother you,
            and nothing can do anything with you,
                if there's anything is going to be bad,
                    you will know.
        Then you will get it out from you,
            and you'll be free at all times.
        And sometimes, that I can let you know,
            that you might do something for your people.
        But if I don't tell you,
            don't do things to anyone,
                even if they hurt, or sick or whatever they was.
        Don't do anything unless I let you know.
        If I don't, don't do anything.
        But if I tell you, you can do it."

You know, they tell them
  all about what they should do
    and then tell them,

    "This is the song.
      You sing that song.
      Start to sing that song, then you go back."

She started to sing, seems to know the song already.
And she sing the song and they walk back.
And not too far,
  and she must have fall.
She didn't know.
The first thing she knew, the sun was high.
She sleep there.
And never get home.
She walk away,
  about two, three hundred yards away from that cow,
    then she drop and sleep.
All night,
  and when she wakes up,
    and the sun was up,
      come up a little higher.
And then she all right.
So she walk home, and get there,
  and then pull out that ear,
    that she cut from the cow, ears,
      and give them to her father.
Says,

    "I get there, and I cut this off. Look at it."

So the old man satisfied,
  because he know
    that she get there.
And the old man, he knew that cow
  that she talked to, and
    she got the *shoo*-MISH already.
Because that old man's idea,

   seems like they, they give it to her.
Seems like he give her a note
   to get over there,
      so that dead cow could know that this was given,
      because that old man's power,
         seems to turn it to her for that time,
            but he still had the part of it,
               till he die, then it will be all to her.
And it was.

See?
That's one way to get the power.
That's another, another way,
   that's one way—different.
And the others, I did tell you that,
   they got different way to get 'em.
And this one, that's the way they get 'em.

GETTING TO BE A POWER MAN

A boy is mesmerized by a whirlwind that suddenly becomes a boy who talks to him.

Another boy become to be a power man.
He become to be power man when he gets to be middle-aged,
    something like that.
And by the whirlwind.

> *Wendy: So the whirlwind was his shoo-MISH?*

Right.

> *Wendy: And that made him ha-HA*?*

Yeah.
That the whirlwind, that become to his shoo-MISH.
He found that.

> *Wendy: That made him ha-HA?*

Yeah.
Well, it's not the shoo-MISH.
That is another shoo-MISH.

---

* Harry found this a difficult word to define in English. It seems to connote a magic power inherent in the objects of nature. This power is more potent than the natural power of humans.

Might be ha-HA, may not so much.
Anyway, that boy, he was a good enough to look for horses.
Could be 'round eight or nine years old.
Maybe ten, something like that.
One morning, his dad wake him up early in the morning
    in the summertime.
Like in maybe June or July.
You know, those time, the day was long.
They get daylight early.
Maybe three o'clock, half past two
    when they get daylight.
And his dad wake him up and tell him,

"You get up. And go out and look for the horses."
    Find the horses.
    Some of 'em was hobbled and some of 'em was loose.
    And you find these horses and unhobble 'em
        and you bring all—the whole bunch.
    Ride 'em—you can ride bareback on one of them—
        and you drive the rest of them.
    We can use the horses after a while."

So he went out.
Look for horses.
And he went out, walked for quite a ways,
    and the wind was blowing.
He can feel that the wind was blowing.
And he looked around and he could see that whirlwind,
    you know.
They could see 'em spinning,
    and they pick up the dust, you know.
And they raise,
    not very big.
But he sees that, and it going kind of fast.
Looks like somebody running.
He watch 'em and then he looked
    and then he see another one.
He see 'em—same way.
There seems to be somebody running.
And he watch 'em.

And he was walking but stopped,
  and he just stood there and watch 'em.

And he went around
  and he go that way
    and then he make a circle the other way.
And around, and come back that way.
Pretty soon it come towards him, you know.
He was still standing there and it clear.
It wasn't until he get close—
  just about like you—
    they were that close.
In a second, and there was another boy.
Just like him.
Another boy.
First, in the first place,
  they thought that was a whirl, the wind, a whirlwind,
    running.
But by the time they get close,
  they can come to him.
And they thinks they were another boy.
Just like him.

And he told 'em,

  "Well, boy, you're here.
    Early in the morning."

He says, "Yeah."

And he told 'em,

  "I'm just another boy.
    I been running around—
      you see me—I been running around.
    I was so happy—early in the morning.
    I running around.
    I was so happy, I run over the things.
    Anything I run over, they raise way up in the air.
    Anything I run over, they will raise.

I was so happy, and I running around.
And then I see you.
And I thought that was another boy.
Maybe I better talk to him—
    going to be my friend."

That's what the whirlwind told 'em.
They change to another boy.
So they told 'em,

    "From now on, sing the song.
        Sing the song."

And tell 'em,

    "I sing the song, and you sing.
        We'll both sing, right here.
        We both sing the song."

For a while, and the—the whirlwind told 'em,

    "That's going to be your power
            and later on, when you get to be a man,
                sometimes you might be worried or something.
        You might worry or might kind of scared or something.
        Maybe something's going to be wrong
            or something like that,
                and it's going to be bad for you.
        If you happen to be that way, you kind of think.
        Now we get together, and they could think of this song
            and then you could sing this song
                early in the morning.
        Early in the morning, you don't have to run like I do.
        But you can walk 'round in the lonely place.
        Nobody around—you can go out way, way out
            where nobody around.
        And you can walk around, but make kind of a circle.
        And you might kind of kick or something
            and makes kind of a dust.
        Kick the ground or something else

so the dust, it'll raise.
Walk around and sing this song.
Then for a while, and then you go back.
And after that, it wouldn't be long,
   and all this what you worrying about it
      and what you worrying for,
         or what you scared for—
            they'll be go away from you.
They'll be disappeared.
And that will be okay.
There's nothing can do anything with you
   when you sing this song
      and walk around early in the morning.
Just like we do now."

So that's what they told him.
Then, tell 'em,

   "Sing the song."

He sing the song.
And tell 'em,

   "All right. I leave you."

And he see 'em—see 'em run.
It was a boy.
But just little ways, just in the second,
   and they see that whirlwind.
It goes the same way.
They spin the dust and way up.
And they go a little ways
   and then they just go off and then fall.

Now, when this boy—when they get bigger, you know,
   when they comes to be a man
      and they pretty near almost middle-aged,
         they still remember.
Once in a while, they sing that song.
But, one night and they could hear that song.

Hear that song.
Somebody think somebody sing that song.
And he go with them
  and he sing the song.
It was that way for three, four night.
Not every night, but like every other night or two.
And he hear that song
  and he sing with 'em.

But finally, one night, and he told 'em,

  "Now, that was me.
    Remember, we get together—"

Tell him which place.

  "In the certain place we get together.
    And I told you this.
    And now is time for you to have it.
    From now on, anytime that you worried about something,
      and you can do as I tell you.
    And if, what it worries you,
      or if you got sick and you can worry about—
        something like that.
    Remember this and then you can do as I tell you.
    And then you get over it."

He let 'em know.
He tell 'em.
So after that, if they get worried for something,
  or sick or supposing if they going to get in jail
    or go for trial or something,
      anybody can worry about that, you know.
And they could sing that song
  and go out in early in the morning by himself
    and walked around.
Not too long, and no more.
That's all they can do.
They don't have to use that for someone—
  to help anybody with his power.

But just for his own.
And that's another one.
Don't seems to be very much but that's one of 'em anyway.
So that's all about that.

WHEN THEY GET TOGETHER, THEY JUST LIKE AN ANIMAL

Two young people, left alone by their families in the mountains to train, accidentally meet.

Now we go to another one.
That's a longer stories.
Not too long, but it's longer than Andrew's stories
    and Charlie's stories.
And that's a long, long time,
    before there ever was a white man around in this area.
There might've been some
    but they might've been way back in the east.
Not here, not around here.
No white man,
    just nothing but Indians in this area.
Right down to Brewster, at that time.
Long time ago.
I couldn't say what year
    but there is no white man at all in this area.
In the west.
But might be in the back east, you know.
Around Nova Scotia or New Brunswick
    and along that place, you know.
At that time.
But it takes a few years, quite a few years,

to come here.
Just a few.
So, that's a long time ago.

And there was a lot of Indians lived at Brewster.
Now the white people call that Brewster.
But they used to call that in Indian name,
    Ko-RA-tin.
That means, one little mountain,
    they is nothing but yellow.
Like sunflower in springtime.
That's why they call that Ko-RA-tin.
See, they yellow.
In English, they say yellow.
But in Indian, in Okanagan word,
    they call 'em grey.
See, the sunflower they are grey in my language.
And that's why they call them Ko-RA-tin.
Means, the whole little mountain,
    they nothing but yellow with the sunflower.
Where the town is now, on that side.
But just little mountain.
In springtime when the sunflower,
    they come in bloom,
        and that little mountain,
            they just a yellow.
You could see it from a long ways.
That's why they call it Ko-RA-tin.
In another name, they call it N-kli-kum-CHEEN.
That means the two water gets together,
    the Columbia River and the Okanagan River.
The Okanagan River they call that river over there.
The Similkameen River and they joins the Okanagan.
But from there, is only Okanagan.
Till they gets to the Columbia River.
The Similkameen River, they disappear,
    right there in Oroville.
That time.
Well, even today it's the same way.

And that time, a lot of Indians at Brewster.
The some of them, they live just where the town is now.
And some of them, they live in the two river
  where they gets together,
    in this side, in the west side,
      I mean in east side of the Okanagan River
        where they gets together.
That's some of the Indian, they live there.
They like two bunches.
Maybe three bunches.
Maybe some others somewhere else, you know.
A lot of Indian.
And these Indians, they come this way,
  they come a little bit this way,
    come up the river.
And they go up to—
  they call it Methow.
That's a big creek,
  runs into the Columbia River.
The other side of Brewster.
They call that, now call it, Bateres.
That place.
Little town.
That big creek runs in there,
  in the Columbia River.
And that's where the Indians from Brewster,
  not far but just a little ways,
    and they go up that creek.
All the way, way up to the mountain.
All the way to the creek.
And way up there,
  they call it Methow.
Now, there's a lot of white people up there.
Big ranches.
They got a little town in places.
But those days, they nothing.
Only the goat and the bear and the wild sheep
  and the deer and all animals
    and all digging and all berries.
That's all they had.

That's where the Indians go up there
    to get those.
For food for the winter.

In the winter, in the fall,
    they go down in the bottom.
Where there's not much snow.
In the winter.
And they spend the winter at the bottom.
At the river.
But up there, there's a lot of snow
    because it's higher.
But when the snow goes off up there,
    in the summer,
        they move.
They stay up there all summer.
And they kept a-going,
    and way up to the top at the timber line
        on the ridge—
            and that's the big ridge between Columbia River
                and the coast.
It's a long ways, but that's the big ridge.
High.
They get up there in the month of August
    maybe, sometimes,
        and they hunt a deer,
            a big deer, you know,
                they fat up there.
A lot of 'em.
They always do.

And one man, supposed to be chief,
    chief of the drive.
He's the chief.
And he got the son.
He got only one son.
Or, he might be the oldest son,
    but they might have some more,
        but they young, you know.
But that's the oldest son.

But only one, anyway.
They were up there, not only him,
  but there's these other people.
Bunch of them.
They were up on top.
In between Columbia River and the coast.
Right on top of the high mountain.
Big country.
They huntin' big deer.
Buck, you know.
Lot of deer.
And they camp there for, oh, three weeks, maybe.
Four weeks.
And then they go back.

And this boy, his son,
  gettin' to be about—
    could be about eighteen years old.
He's good enough to get along by himself.
That is, if they were alone.
Eighteen years old, is getting to be a man then.
When they were up there, and he said to his son,

  "After a while, we go over there."

And he mention whereabout, the place.
There is supposed to be a lake.
Nice place.

  "We going to make a winter camp in there.
    We going to make a good winter camp.
    Winter house, like.
    Not *kekuli* house,★ but fix 'em,
      they can be used for winter."

And his son told 'em,

★ Kekuli house refers to the winter home used by the Okanagan until the mid-nineteenth century. Known in English as a pithouse, it was dug partially into the ground for protection and warmth.

"Why did we have to make a winter house over there?"
He says,

"That's just the way.
    We got to make it."

And the young man, he was still wondering,
    what was he going to make the winter house
      on top of the summit?
But anyway, they go over there
    and then they built the winter house.
They built 'em good.
And they cover 'em so it can be good
    even if it's cold.
And there's a lot of wood.
They bring a lot of wood.
When they finish, then it's getting to be about time
    for these people to go back down.

And he says to his boy,

"We finished this winter house.
    And that's going to be yours.
    You're going to stay there.
    You're not going down with us.
    We're going down, but not you.
    When we go down, you stay there.
    You stay there for the winter.
    All winter you stay right here.
    Next year about this time,
      we'll come up again.
    Then we'll meet you.
    You could still [be] here the next year."

So the boy, he don't seems to like it that way
    because, way back in the mountain
      and he got to be all alone.
But his dad say so.
And his grandfather.
They all agree that way.

His mother, his grandmother, all them.
They got to be there.
All right, he thought to themself,

    "Okay, I'll stay.
        Whether I make it through the winter or not,
        but I'll stay anyway."

He thought.
So, in a few days they left.
And this young man, he was there by himself.
And he's good enough to hunt, you know.
He got the bow and arrow,
    he got a knife, and
        he have everything that they need.
He can hunt and then he can get the deer
    and then he can cut 'em in pieces
        and then he can dry 'em.
He know that.
He know how.
He's old enough to know everything.
But he's kind of young.

So he was there.
He hunt.
And then he get deer
    and then he dry 'em
        and then he put 'em away for the winter
           and he look around
               and he could find the wild potatoes.
In places they go downhill a bit somewhere,
    and they dig that,
        and bring 'em
        and keep 'em there.
So he could use that in the winter.
There is quite a few things that he get.
So he could use that for him to eat
    for all the winter.
So he stay there.
He stay there till one years.

And he kind of think
   maybe his folks is going to come at any time,
      it's about time to come.
So he think,

   "I'm going away.
      When they do come,
         they're not going to see me.
      I'm not going to be here when they get here."

So he left.
He figured he look at the country
   and he would be going that way quite a ways,
      you know, he might walk for a couple days
        and camp over there,
           quite a ways.
And he know the country.
So he thought,

   "I'm going the north.
      Straight north.
      I'm going long ways.
      So they never find me.
      They can miss me."

But that's what they want 'em to be.
So he left.
He come up, right on the ridge
   and he go quite a ways to the north.
Then, his folks, a bunch of people, come.
Then they stop there for a while
   and then they kept a-coming.
So they thought,

   "We going to see the boy."

He is supposed to be there.
But when they come to that winter house,
   he not there.
So they thought he might've walk away,

he might stay over there for a couple of days
  and he'll be back.
And they kind of expect him to get back,
  but never get back.
They don't see him.
They stay there long time,
  about a month.
And he never get back.
And they were wondering why.
They thought maybe he go someplace,
  maybe grizzly bear killed 'em.
Maybe a cougar or something.
They missed 'em.
So finally, they couldn't stay there.
Getting late.
They got to go back down.

So they went back.
They don't know where the boy was.
They never seen him.
But this boy, he begin to have a power
  because he been there alone a long time.
And he have a power already.
And he knew,
  his people, they go back.
So finally, he know for sure
  they went quite a ways back.
They can't come back.
So he went back.
And he get to that place
  and stay there for another winter.
Stay there till springtime.
Stay there end of summer.
And, pretty soon their folks is going to come.
He go away again.
And he stay away, way up north
  because he know the country.
Way far.
And these people, they were around
  for a while, still missin' 'em.

But in the first time,
　　when they get back down,
　　　in the winter,
　　　　they put up a powwow.
And there was some Indian doctor in this bunch, you know.
Lots of 'em.
And they sing their song
　　and they look for him by their power.
And they find out he was around,
　　but not there.
He was alive, and he was around,
　　but long way.
To the north.
So they tell the old man, the old people,

　　"Your son is alive.
　　　But not there.
　　　He went quite a ways.
　　　But, might come back."

And he did come back, you know,
　　in that winter house.
But next year, pretty soon they come up.
These other people.
They go away again.
And these people around there,
　　till they're ready to go back.
And they go back.

Then, he was there two winters.
And on the second, he was there one year,
　　when they left the girl,
　　　that's from the other side,
　　　　that's from the coast.
The people they do the same thing,
　　they come up from the coast,
　　　way up on top of that place,
　　　　just like these people do.
So these people, the next year,
　　the one year that boy was there,

and they come up . . .
They always come up
  but they don't meet,
    they don't see each other.
So, they do the same.
They left the girl in that area.
Not exactly the same place where that boy was,
  but in that area.
In the ridge, you know.
So this girl, she spent a winter there.
The whole winter.
And that's one year for her,
  and two years for the boy, in the same area.
They left 'em there,
  just like they do with the boy.
But, sometimes in the summer,
  and this girl seems to go up north a ways.
And this other one, that boy,
  he seems to go back that way.
And finally, I don't know which one,
  either the boy or the girl—
    I think the girl was—
      seen the tracks.
Person.
Man or man, or maybe a woman.
Anyway, there's somebody,
  it's a person's tracks.
Not bear.
A person's tracks.
No shoes those days, just moccasins.
See the tracks.
In the culvert.
Build, you know, the culvert.
They dig the ground and they build 'em up.
And he step on that
  and then she could see the tracks.
And she think, must've be somebody round here.
And every time she seems to look around
  to see if she might seen them.
And the boy, he get going that way

and pretty soon he see tracks.
Same as the girl.
He seen the tracks,
  he looked at the tracks,
    and he kind of watch 'em
      and he follow the tracks
        and looked around
          and he seen 'em again once in a while.

  "By God, they not pretty big tracks.
    My God, these tracks,
      it looks like a woman tracks."

So they begin to look for it.
They both of 'em.
The girl they looking for who's got the tracks there.
And the boy they do the same thing.
They look for whose tracks is that.
Pretty soon they—not right away—
  but takes a while
    and they found one another.
But the boy, he's the one that see the girl first.
He seen 'em from the distance.
Seen her, she was going.
And, by God, he thinks,

  "If I go over there, like fast,
    and if they see me,
      they might run
        and I could never catch 'em.
  I better sneak around
    and go around in front of 'em
      and seems to be go right around."

Because he got the power already.
If they do, if they go in a circle then,
  go right around her,
    they seems to catch 'em
      and then hold 'em.
And then they can keep sneak around, till he get close.

Then let 'em know.
So she wouldn't run away.
So he do that.
He seen 'em
   but he went off the side
      and then he make the circle
         and then he walk a long ways
            and they make a circle.
And he knows, she's still around there.
And he get closer
   and he keep going,
      sneaked, you know.
Till he get pretty close.
And the girl never seen 'em,
   but she seen the tracks.
She was wondering,
   she still look.
Somebody talk to her.
She look.
He's not far.
As soon as she could see it was another person,
   a man, not far,
      well, then she couldn't run.
She know right away it was a person.
So they met together.
And, they were together.
They ask one another,

   "How long you been here?"

The boy said that,

   "This is the two years I been here."

And the girl says,

   "This is one year I been here."

All right.
They not too long.

And they get together.
And then they—
That's his wife, you know, that way.
And they, they always together.
And they, the boy said,

"My people is coming pretty soon."

And she said, her people they were coming.

The boy said,

"I always go away.
    I don't want them to see me."

So the girl said,

"That's a good idea.
    Let's go.
    To heck with 'em."

So they went to the north,
    the both of 'em.
But these other people from the coast,
    they come look for the girl—that's one year there.
They thought they could find her,
    but not.
But these other people—
    that's the third year, like—
        they never see the boy,
            but they know he were alive.
By their power.
But they know he go way up north.
They couldn't catch up to 'em.

So these people, they were there,
    all together, the boy—
    five years there on the mountain.
And the girl—
    like four years there.

And then the girl says—
  not the girl—
    the boy says,

    "Maybe we'd better go to your people."

He tell the girl,

    "We go down.
      To your people.
      And we stay there.
      Maybe we stay there two years.
      Maybe three years.
      Then we come back here.
      If we want we can stay here for another couple of years.
      And then we go to my people."

So they went.
From there they went to the coast.
They go down,
  go down,
    go down.
And this girl was missing.
They seems to be year after that.
And this girl was missing.
They know they up there in the first year.
But in the second year they missing them.
They do the same.
They sing the song and they find out,
  she's up there.
She's alive.
She's got somebody with 'em.
She not only one.
By now they were two.
And this other one,
  they find that out.
They know they found the one another.
And they're two now.
They know.

But they went down to the girl's people.
In about three years' time.
Two years.
And they get down there kind of early in the fall.
So they were there.
They lived there for two years.
And the boy says,

　　"Well now, we've been here long enough.
　　　　Two years with your people.
　　　　We'll go up on the mountain.
　　　　And maybe we spend one year there,
　　　　　　before we go to my people."

All right.
They tell the woman's people.
So they went up.
And they get up to that place
　　because they know all that place.
So finally they spend about two years.
They like it because they get used to it.
But, they went down to Brewster,
　　to the boy's people.
So, like he was away for about seven years.
But he get down.
He had a wife
　　and they had a little boy,
　　　　like you got, you know.
When they get to his people, you know.
But they both of 'em
　　real good Indian doctors.
The both of 'em.
Because the boy was alone in that mountain two years.
And the girl was alone there one year.
But when they get together,
　　they just like an animal,
　　　　the both of 'em.
And the boy, maybe they go out by himself
　　to hunt, or something like that.

Or the girl, goes out to get some berries
  or something, by herself.
And still they meet the animals
  and talk to 'em.
By this time, they get down to the boy's people,
  and they were real power persons,
  the both of 'em.
Good Indian doctor.

And they were there for about three years.
And they go back to the other place.
They do that,
  back and forth.
They stay in one place two years.
Then they go back to the other place.
Spend there two years.
They kept doing that till they get old.
And they done a lot of work.
There are a lot of sick people,
  they go to work on them
    and they get them better.
In this place.
And in the same way at the other place
  when they were over there.
They real good Indian doctor.
They got all kinds of power.
And they know everything.
They can tell.
They can tell you what's going on ahead
  in a week or so, or few days, or—
They know everything.
It's just like they seen everything.
They real good.

See, that's the way the Indian get this power
  in another way.
That's another way to get their power.
They work for it, you know.
They go to get it.
See, that's a long time they be on the mountain,

all alone.
See, that's the reason I always say, the Indian,
    they were different than the white.
Because the white people,
    they could never do that, I don't think.
They could spend a winter for trapping,
    and like that, you know,
        but they always gets home.
But this Indian, they stay there.
So, that's the stories about that.

I heard that stories,
    but I cannot remember who tell me.
Someone—
I think Shmit-KUN-tin was telling me that.
And Charlie Jim.
Either one of them,
    or else maybe the both of 'em.
I think.
I think the both of 'em tell me.
They both know that
    because they live there.
And one of 'em started to tell me,
    but the other one, they knows about
        then he seems to help the other one.
Telling me.
Shmit-KUN-tin and Charlie Jim.
These is the mans that tell me about that.
But they both died.
Shmit-KUN-tin, he died.
And Charlie Jim, he died.
So—but I still remember that story.
That's over there.
So that's the story.

PART II

POWER JUST FOR
THEMSELVES

DON'T TAKE ME
TO A DOCTOR!

Injured while bronco-riding, George Hanes instructs his friends to take him into the woods and leave him there and not to return until the following morning.

George Hanes, his name was, the man.
He died in '74.
He's a little older than me.
He got hurt one time.
In Omak.
He had a rodeo, long time ago.
At that time, maybe the first rodeo,
    maybe the second rodeo in Omak.
And they got, they fall off, get bucked off,
    and they got caught in stirrup.
And they was hanged on the side of the horse
    and the horse whirl around and around
        and kicked 'em.
And he kicked 'em in the body.
And broke the ribs.
Badly hurt.
And finally they—
    the other cowboys—
        they get the horse.
They got 'em.
And they had to cut the leather cord, you know,
    to get the saddle off the horse

because his feet was caught in the stirrups.
And they couldn't get them off.
They cut the leather cord, and it come off.
Takes his feet out, and he was badly hurt.
All his chest—here—and his back.
Broken ribs.
In the afternoon, about four o'clock in the afternoon,
   when it happened.
Then they told him,

    "Well, we should take you—
        we goin' to take you to a doctor.
      Take you to hospital."

Doctor, anyway.
I think there's no hospital that time.
But there was doctor.

    "Take you to doctor."

He said,

    "No.
      Don't take me to a doctor."

He says,

    "You could put me on the buggy.
      On one-horse buggy.
      And take me over the road,
        and take me up the river a ways."

This a bushy land.
Now the highway it's there.
As you go from here
   you cross the river and to your left—
      it's still kind of bushy land in there.
That's from the rodeo ground.
And he says,

"Take me over there.
    Take my saddle along,
        and my saddle blanket,
            and my bridle and my rope,
                and left me over there where is nobody there.
    Left me there and come back.
    And don't go over there until tomorrow
        till the sun is way, 'round about nine, ten o'clock,
            and then you can go and see me.
    If I'm there."

All right.
He's badly hurt, and they take him to the camp
    and they bring the one-horse buggy, you know,
        and they put 'em in the buggy.
Load him there, and they haul him over there.
Take his saddle along, and his blanket.
They take him on the buggy
        and take him over there.
In that strange place.
Just a bushy land.
The brush, you know, not very high.
Just small, but it's a bushy land.
So they left 'em there.
In about four o'clock, or half past four,
    something like that,
        they left 'em there.
And they all come back.

The next morning the sun was up
    about nine o'clock.

    "Well," they say,
    "Let's go and see our friend.
        Maybe he's dead."

So, the two, three man and they went over there.
When they get near,
    Mr. Hanes, he was sitting,

his saddle was laying there,
and he was sitting,
kind of laying against the saddle.
And he was sitting there, singing his song.
And when they get there and they told 'em,

"Well, George, you—you all right?"

"Oh yeah. I'm gettin' all right."

"Yeah, well, maybe we should take you to the camp."

"Yeah. All right."

He get up.

"You don't have to carry me on the buggy.
I go."

He walked over there.
When they get to the cabin, they get the big rag,
tie 'em up, like.
And he was there alone, all night.
And then his, his bird, or animal, whatever,
they talked to him when he was little boy,
he come there, they come there and fix 'em up.
Or else he might've,
throw out the blood.
And he get better.
Then he's all right.
I never seen that done,
but the people talked about it.
A lot of people talked about it.
George Hanes is well known.
He's quite a man.
He's quite a guy.
He's a bronc rider and he's all-round cowboy.

THROW ME IN
THE RIVER

*After accidentally injuring himself with a knife, a man insists that his
companions throw him into the Thompson River.*

Did I ever tell you?
What I was going to say?
Oh, I think I did tell you,
   or maybe not—
      the fella that cut his leg with a knife, in Kamloops.
He cut, a butcher knife.
And he supposed to cut the tail of the cows,
   not the whole thing, but only the hair.
You know, the tail and the end of the bone tail,
   but the long hair from that—
Just the hair.
And he cut those hair, only.
Bobtail the cows, that they can be marked,
   more like a brand.

He was doing that.
There three, four of them, riders.
And one of the boys, he was drinkin'.
And he grabbed the cow's tail—
Maybe the cow is that way and he grabbed the tail
   and he cut 'em with a knife
      but he had the tail too far up
         and he cut above his knees.
About there.

Cut 'em with a knife.
Sharp knife.
And he cut 'em right to the bone.
And a long cut, about that long.
And when he cut 'em,
     and the skin was open up and bleed.
Bleed quite a bit, you know.
They bleed.
Still on the horse.
And this man, is not full Indian.
He's half-white and half-Indian.
But still, he's on his Indian side.
His idea.
When he had that cut, and that's bad.
Liable to die because the blood was—
     too much losing blood.
And he said to the others,

          "My friend, help me.
          Take me and get me off the horse
               and get a heavy canvas.
          And put me in canvas the four of you.
          Each one can be in a corner of the canvas.
          And take me to the Thompson River.
          And you could swing me two, three times,
               and then throw me in the river.
          Then I'll be floating down,
               about a mile down below.
          And I'll get out of the river,
               and there was some trees just there
                    and I can be sitting there.
          Wait for you guys.
          Watch the sun.
          The sun when it gets way over, 'bout two, three o'clock
               in the afternoon,
                    then you could drive the buggy over."

There no car those days, no nothing.
Just only single-horse buggy.

"Drive the buggy over there
    and then you bring me.
Put me on the buggy and bring me.
And then you could take me to a doctor,
    and then the doctor could sew that.
But if you don't, I'm liable to die."

All right.
The others,

"Okay, we'll do that."

But the others, they said,

"No, don't do that.
Why do you have to throw 'em in the river?
You not do that.
You should not supposed to throw 'em in the river.
Thompson River.
Big river.
They raisin' too."

Some Indians, and some white people,
    but some of 'em, they run up to town
        to tell the policeman and doctor.
They run over there to report.
But the others, is going to him to throw 'em in the river.
But the others, they don't want it that way.
But the others said,

"All right.
    Throw 'em in the river."

So, two ways, right there.
Anyhow, these others,
    they pick up a canvas and they lead the horse out there
        and they pull him off the horse
            and put 'em on the canvas.
Four man, and one man on each corner of the canvas.

See? The canvas, they had four corners.
Big canvas.
Heavy canvas.
And they run to the river.
And the others tell 'em,

"Don't do that.
    Don't do it."

But they keep going.
And when they get to the edge of the river,
    there was a little bank, you know,
        they get to the river to the water.
And they swing 'em.
And he sing a song, that man is on the canvas.
And these others, they sing the song too.
And they swing him few times.
At last, they throw 'em.
They tip the canvas over,
    these other who raise it high.
And, they throw 'em in the river.
And they could see 'em, when they get in the river.
And they could see 'em turning over.
They floating over.
Turn in the water.
Turning over by water.
And then they come back and had that canvas.
But they reported to the police and doctor.
They not coming yet.
But man, who's got hurt, he floating down.

After little while, the whole bunch come.
The two, three policeman and two, three doctor.
Two doctor, anyway.
When they come, this bunch is just standing round.

"Where is that man that got hurt?"

This one and that one too, says,

"We put 'em on the canvas and throw 'em in the river.
   We watching 'em and they floating."

And, by God, the policeman, you know,
   they going to handcuff them, everyone.
But there was talker from the bunch.
Says,

"Policeman, just a minute.
   Let me tell you something.
   Don't be too rushed."

So finally they—and the first word they talks to 'em—
   and they talks to 'em good.
So the policeman would stop and listen.
And tell 'em. He said,

"We trying to save our friend.
   We throw 'em in the river so we could save life.
   We could save him better.
   We don't want to lose him.
   We want him to get better.
   He's a pretty good hand.
   He's a pretty good cowhand.
   We want him.
   We throw him in the river.
   That's how it is.
   This is a power man.
   He'll come back."

And the policeman tells 'em,

"Maybe you better go down,
      go find 'em and bring 'em."

He says,

"No.
   We know what time we can go and get 'em.

He's going to come out of the river at certain place.
He's going to sit by the tree, against the tree.
Till a certain time, and we get there.
And we bring 'em on the buggy,
    and we take him right on through to a doctor.
And let the doctor sew him.
If you policeman want to see 'em,
    you could see him.
But that's what we're going to do.
We know.
We wait till its time comes."

So they give 'em a good talking
    and the policeman give up.
All right.

    "All right.
        We want to say,
            'Well, you can go to a doctor office.
            And when you get him there,
                and the doctor lets you know,
                    you can come and see.'"

All right.
They leave.
They wait till the sun gets there.
'Bout three, four o'clock.
They took the buggy over there.
About a mile or more down the river.
Was a road, all the way.
When they get there,
    he sitting against the tree on his back.
Singing a song.
His song.
His power song.

When the boys get near,
    then he stopped singing.
Then he hold 'em and let them set 'em on the buggy.
And then they take 'em to a doctor.

Get them to the doctor
  and the doctor called the policeman.
Said,

    "The man that got hurt —"

Said,

    "They were here now.
      Come and see 'em."

After a little while the policeman come.
And take a look.
And that's all.
Write it down.

So, the doctors sewed him.
Finish him, and the doctor says,

    "Has to go to a hospital."

This man, the one that got hurt, says,

    "No.
      I'm not going to hospital.
      I'm going back to my own bunk.
      And I can stay in my own bunk.
      And I'm not going to hospital.
      I don't want that hospital.
      I go back to my own bed
        and stay there till I get better.
      And then I can use my own medicine."

They give 'em some medicine,
  they can use that all right,
    but he got to use some of the Indian medicine.
Not only the white man medicine.
He can use the Indian medicine too.
So, they get 'em that way.
They take 'em home.

And they put 'em on his own bed.
Somebody watching 'em.
Somebody there, or somebody get some food
   and take it to him and stay there.
A few days.
And then they go on the crutch.
Not very long,
   and then they healed up.
And then they go to doctor, and doctor says,

   "Well, it's getting to be better
      but watch 'em for a while."

And not too long, about a month or six weeks,
   he's on the horse.
Cowboying again.
See, you can see the difference
   between the white and the Indian.
There are a lot of difference.
They not all the same.
And this man is half-Indian and half-white,
   but he's—he's Indian side.
Claimed himself was an Indian.
That's the way it goes.

A POWER MAN, HE KNOWS WHAT'S COMING TO HIM

A rodeo man predicts his own demise.

Joe Harris.
His name's Joe Harris,
  he lives in Omak.
Young man.
He's about ten years younger than me,
  Joe Harris.
His name, Joe.
And his dad, his name—
  well, his dad's name is—
    he's that too,
      his name, Harry.
Like my first name, Harry.
But to some people,
  they call him Joe Harry.
Well, pretty soon
  the others, they call him Joe Harris.
That sounds like a name, but—
  sounds like the same.
It's much easier to say that.
So they always called Joe Harris
  just all by himself for that story alone.
He's only young man,
  he died in 1950 at the rodeo,

at the rodeo in Brewster.
They had a rodeo,
  Joe Kelsey
    he run the rodeo at Brewster
      at that time.
And Joe Harris,
  he's one of the
    almost top rider.
Good rider.
But he's not the top
  but—near.
He good rider, anyway.
He always go to rodeo,
  and he always ride the saddle bronc,
    or, bareback, and things like that.
He's a cowboy.
But one time
  he always say,
    he always say he's a power man.
He tell the other people,
  and they always say that,
    and then they think
      he seems to be higher than anybody.
He said he's a power man,
  he can do anything.
He always say that.
But there was some other Indian doctor
  they got jealous at him from saying that.
And they give 'em a power
  so he could die that way.
Because he always say,

  "I'm a good rider.
    I'm a really good rider,
      wouldn't be long
    I'll be the winner.
    I'm coming to.
    Getting better,
      getting better."

They mention that to all people—
    not all, but most of them.
But some Indian doctor, they
    don't like that kind of a word,
        to hear somebody saying that.
And they give 'em that power.
And they said,

> "That man.
>   He was a bronc rider.
>   He was good—he's going to be good
>   later on.
>   We know.
>   But he's going to die that way.
>   He's going to die on the bronc riding.
>   Next rodeo, he's going to die."

He knows!
He was a power man.
He know what's coming to him.
But what he can do?
Nothing.
But he know.
And he said,
    he said to the people,

> "When the rodeo comes
>   and all the horses get there,
>   and then the rodeo started.
>   Can be two days' rodeo.
>   And all the cowboys,
>   all the cowboys,
>   or even not cowboys,
>   but a lot of people there."

And he was there,
    well he was—
        he's supposed to ride.
And the others,

the other riders, they know.
They all know him.
And they met him.

They say,

    "Hello, Joe."

    "Hello."

    "Are you going to ride this time?"

    "Oh, sure.
      I always ride.
      But I'll tell you something.
      I'm going to ride this time
        whenever my turn comes.
      Then I'll get on the saddle bronc.
      But I will never come back.
      I'm going to fall off out in the arena
        or somewhere.
      And I'll be there—
        never come back."

    "What do you mean?"

    "I'm going to die wherever I fall."

    "Ah!"

They laugh at him.
And he said,

    "All right, shake hand, my friend.
      That's from my death.
      I'm going to die
        whenever I bucked off.
      I'm going to die."

And the others,
   they tell him,

   "Why, you shouldn't ride
      if you think it's that way."

   "Yes," he said,
   "I'm supposed to ride.
    I'm a rider,
    I'm not going to back out.
    I'm going to die that way."

But the people,
   they think he's just a-joking.
He say that for fun, they think.
Teasing,
   because he always say things like that.
They give a lot of joke about him.
He's a good power man.
So this time they think
   he's doing that.
But he mean it.
And nobody seems to know.

So he met this other one,
   he say the same thing.

   "Well, Joe,
      you going to ride?"

   "Oh yeah.
    I always ride.
    But whenever my turn comes
    I'll ride and never come back
      from where I fall off."

He say the same thing to several of them.
And they shook hands.

"That's for my death."

And they just look at him,
  shake hands anyway.
And then the announcer mention his name,

    "This is Joe's horse,
      Joe Harry."

Okay.
Put the horse in the chute
  and he walked
    that way,
      and whoever they met
        on his way
          going to the chute
            shake hand this one
              and there and there—

  "Good-bye, my friend.
    I get on, and
        never come back."

And then he get on that horse,
  and he said.

We always—
I work that place, you know.
And we always watch the rider,
  and we hold 'em on the belt, you know,
    in case if the horse rear up
      we can help 'em getting off sooner.
And the guider there,
  the one that helps,
    they hold 'em and
      tell 'em,

    "Be careful."

    "I'll be careful all right."

But he's going to die when he go out.
So they ready.
All right.

    "Good-bye, my friends,
      good-bye!"

Open the door,
  and away they go.
The horse were
  big horse.
Great big, stout.
And he bucked quite a ways,
  about six jump.
And then he fall off towards the head, you know,
  rolled over the head
    and landed on the ground,
      and this horse jump on him—
And he seems to
  dance on him, twice.
And he bucked that way
  for one more jump, or two
    and turn around straight back
      and jump on him again
        and dance right on 'em.
Before the others get there
  to stop the horse,
    but they can't stop it,
      they doing it—
        too late to stop him.

They run.
But it's out in the ring, you know.
They have it in a tent.
Before the people get there,
  he's dead.
All smashed,
  all smashed.
He said he'll die

right there where they fall off,
and then it was.

Wendy: And he knew that by his power?

Yeah.
He knew that by his power.
He knew that ahead of time.
Maybe several,
   several days, or—
      maybe several weeks
         he know that ahead of time,
            it's going to happen
               with him.
But he cannot get away.

See?
That's another power way.
He's a power man, but—
   he can tell what's coming to him
      in a certain time.
But he can't stop it,
   he can't beat it.
So he die that way,
   by the other power's order.
See, that's one of them,
   that's about the end of Joe Harris.

THE DEAD MAN,
HE COME ALIVE

A man uses his power to overcome death on three occasions.

His name Charlie,
   Charlie Ya-kum-DI-kin.
That's his name.
That Ya-kum-DI-kin, that's an Indian word.
But Charlie, that's a white man name.
Then Charlie Ya-kum-DI-kin, they have that,
   that's his Indian name, that Ya-kum-DI-kin.
But, they use that,
   they took that for his last name.
By right, it would be Charlie Seymour.
But, they don't call that Seymour.
They call that his Indian name only.
For his last name.
That's how it is.

Anyway, he died.
And then he come alive.
And he died again.
And then he come alive.
He died twice.
And then he was alive a long time
   after the second time he died.
And then he was still alive for long time.
And he died when he's eighty-one.
Got killed, you know.

He got killed in car.
The car run over him.
Him and his horse,
   the both of 'em died,
      that last time.
But he died twice before that.

And I can tell you how come he died in the first place.
They were moving the pack train from Princeton to Hope,
   you know.
They go to Hope.
And the supplies, they comes from Vancouver
   on the same boat.
And come to Hope.
And they unload 'em there.
Because they same boat,
   they can't go any farther up the Fraser River
      because from Hope up is rough.
No sailboats can go that way.
And they can only haul the stuff from Vancouver
   as far as Hope.
Then they unload some on the way,
   on these little towns, you know,
      between Hope and Vancouver.

But anyway, they come as far as Hope.
At those days, long time ago.
And, the Allison, he's the manager for the supply
   to come into Princeton
      and down as far as Rock Creek.
They can be packed, you know,
   as far as Rock Creek.
That's his contract.
And then maybe somebody else from Penticton,
   to join into Penticton to bring the supply
      and go into Penticton.
Those days, you know, on the packhorses.

And Ya-kum-DI-kin, he's got a brother-in-law.
His sister was married to a man,

his name Baptiste.
Baptiste, that's only name I knew.
They might've had a second name
　　but I don't remember that.
But that was his first name.
Baptiste.
And Baptiste, he is the boss, like.
He is the straw boss,
　　for the pack train.
But he's working for Allison.
Allison is the head boss, you know,
　　for the pack train.
But they don't go.
He writes all the paper about them,
　　but they hire a man to handle that.
And they hired that Baptiste
　　to be manager on the pack train.
He was named.
So they went to Hope.
With bunch of packhorses.
I don't know how many.
It might've be—it could be—
　　around fifteen, maybe eighteen, maybe twenty.
Packhorses.
And they were four of them.
Ya-kum-DI-kin and Baptiste and two others.
I don't know the name,
　　but there're four of them.
The packhorses must've been twenty
　　to have that many men to handle 'em.

So, they come over from Hope
　　and they come on the summit
　　　　and they have to stop, you know.
They tooks two nights, from Hope to Princeton.
In the other ways,
　　three days and two nights.
From Hope, they camp.
In the morning from Hope,
　　and that night they camp.

Next day, one day, and they camp again.
The next day they get to Princeton,
  maybe only noon.
Like two days and a half from Hope to Princeton.
When they bring the packhorses.

And the first night they camp, you know,
  comin' from Hope with the packhorses
    with their big packs, you know,
      because they bringin' the stuff,
        the supply from Princeton into Keremeos
          and then they could separate it in Keremeos
            and then they could pack the rest of 'em
              to Rock Creek—
                if they had to.
Sometimes they don't.
Sometimes they makes another trip
  right on through to Rock Creek.
But sometimes they have to take some off
  from this time and leave some in Keremeos
    and then they took the rest of 'em to Rock Creek.
Anyway, they comin' from Hope.
And they camp out the first night on the summit.
And there was some trees,
  something like these trees,
    not pretty big.
But these was a jack pine trees.
And there must've been a fire through there one time
  and all these pine trees just about this size,
    they all dead.
They all dry out.
And it must've been quite a while after they dry out
  and the roots is getting to be kinda rot.
And some of 'em,
  they fall, you know.
They be a few fall.
But some of 'em still standing.
And the new-grown, they just about so high
  already, again.

So they camp there,
  where they had lot of these dry tree.
And they had supper and they make a bed, you know,
  the other man make a bed over there
      and one here
          and they's all over.
Anywhere.
They make a bed.
And they sleep.
Then that night, towards morning,
  about two o'clock in the morning,
      and the wind blows.
It's kind of a storm.
Storm wind.
Rain a little bit,
  and blow hard.
One of the tree,
  about that size, dry one,
      they blow down.
And the tree fall.
And they fall right on the head of Ya-kum-DI-kin.
Just when he's sleeping, you know.
The tree fall right on his head.
And it killed 'em.
And when the wind stopped,
  and they could hear that tree fall.
Just towards him.
So when they go there, in a little while,
  he was just bashed.
Then they stop.
And then they get up, the others,
  and then they look.
And Ya-kum-DI-kin, the tree was on his head.
And they talking, see nothing.
He's dead.
And they make a fire.
There is no flashlight those days.
No barn lantern, no nothing.
See, they have to make a fire
  so they have the light.

And they make a fire
　and make a light
　　and look at 'em.
He's dead.
And they move that tree, you know.
Because they could move—
　they only about that big.
But when they fall, it's heavy, you know.
They hit the man's head
　and they killed 'em.
So they moved the tree.
He's dead.
In early morning, about two o'clock in the morning.

And Baptiste was the boss.
And the two others.

And Baptiste, he says,

　　"We going to cook breakfast.
　　　And coffee and some kind of breakfast.
　　　And we eat.
　　　After we eat, and you two,
　　　　can go to Princeton.
　　　Right from here.
　　　But we leave the horses.
　　　I'll stay right here."

And they see one or two of the horses,
　they come through the fence.
There was a fence there.
But the fence he goes and connect to the bluff.
A little bluff.
But the horses, somehow they broke that.
And they come through.
And they said to the boys,

　　"You two can go to Princeton
　　　and tell our boss one man is dead.
　　And I can stay here.

And then I can put these horses back in there,
  and I find the place where they broke
  and I'm going to fix 'em.
And I look at all the fence.
There might be one more broken somewhere.
And that way the horses will get out and go away.
But you fellas go, early.
So you can get to Princeton before noon.
Should get there about half past ten or eleven,
  in the morning.
And tell the boss.
And they will send a bunch of people,
  in Princeton, whoever they were there,
    some white people, and some Indian.
Maybe it should be several to come.
Several people.
And they can bring some food,
  for them.
Because we got the food
  but it's only enough for one more night.
Till we get to Princeton.
But they can bring their food for them
  when they going to stop here for overnight.
When they come from Princeton,
  maybe in one o'clock in the afternoon,
    maybe two o'clock in the afternoon,
      they come starting from Princeton,
        they will get here just about dark.
And they'll have to stay here for overnight.
But the next morning, early,
  and we'll pack this dead man to Princeton.
And then when we get 'em to Princeton,
  then the other people, his people,
    they will think where he have to be buried.
In the town of Hedley, or Princeton, or where.
But we can take 'em as far as Princeton."

So these two boys, get on the saddle horses
  and then they come.
They come fast, you know.

No nothing to lead, no pack, no nothin'—
   just go on the trail.
Baptiste is still there.
They go over there and then they fix the fence.
They fix that fence and they finish
   and they go back to the camp.
And they pick up some old rope.
They go back to the camp.
And they pick up some rope to use for the other broken,
   if it is.
But at the same time, they look at the dead man.
They kind of thinking, maybe no,
   they might be just knocked out.
They might come alive.
To make sure he really was dead.

So they come back to the camp
   and look at 'em.
They was dead.
They not alive.
Well, all right, he's dead all right.
So they take the rope and then go.
Look for some more broken one,
   fence.
They went out quite a ways
   and they were out there for about an hour or more.
And they come back.
They don't find any.
They all good.
But they come back,
   but it's quite a ways, walking.
And they come back.
At the time when they come back,
   and they just come back out the side
     and they could see he's sitting—
Charlie, he was sitting.

Sitting, and they stop, you know.
Then they wouldn't go no more.
They see him sitting and they stop.

And Charlie, he knows.
They could see, you know,
  and they saw them come.
And they walked over there
  and they said to Charlie,

  "You wake up."

  "Oh yeah.
    I wake up.
    What's the matter?
    What happened with me?
    My head is pretty bad."

And he says,

  "Well, this log, that you were laying
      right there, you know—"

He said,

  "This tree, they fall on your head
      and you was supposed to be in the dead.
    You're knocked out."

When he come alive,
  but his head was all bruised, you know.
All black.
His face all black.

And he said, Charlie said to him,

  "Where's the other boys?"

When they tell him, they said to him,

  "The boys, I sent them to Princeton.
    To tell the people.
    And these people, they might come tonight.
    And tomorrow, if you still dead,

they'll take you to Princeton.
But these boys are going already."

While he saying that, and Charlie told him,

"Maybe we should go.
Get the horses, get our saddle horses,
and we go right now.
We can go fast.
And we can caught up to them people,
they get to the place.
Or else we'll get there,
not too long now till we get there.
So they wouldn't move.
But we don't go,
they be moving this way for nothing."

Well, he said to Charlie,

"You think you good enough to ride?"

"Oh," he said, "I will.
We can ride and we'll go."

"But," he said,
"I might use my medicine on the way going."

So they bring the horses and saddle 'em.
And Charlie, they put up his clothes, you know,
coat and things
and he ride on the horse
and he come down pretty fast on the trail.
And they run for quite a ways.
They run horses, trot them, gallop once in a while
and run, then trot them
for quite a ways.
And they could see the creek.
Small creek.
Well, not too small.
It's a big creek all right.

Not too far from the trail.
Down in the creek, you know.
And the trails is the creek running down.
And it kind of bench,
    and, that's where the trail was.
And they could see the creek.

And Charlie said to him,

> "Maybe we stop here.
>   We stop here and you hold the horses
>   and you stay right here.
>   I'm going down and use my medicine."

And they stop and Charlie get off
    and they went down on the foot.
He walked down to the creek,
    and Baptiste watching him
        and he get to the creek
        and he jump in the creek with his coat
        and everything.

> "Just wait there."

Clothes and all,
    he just lay on the water,
        on the creek.
His head close to the stream.
And one of 'em, his leg,
    and over he goes, over his head, you know.
Lay there for a while.
Then he get up, turn 'round
    and he lay the other way.
And water running in through here.
And Baptiste was watching him,
    like from here across the road here.
That far.

And when he get through,
    and then he come up.

And when he gets here
  and all the water will running
    off through clothes.
And then he get on the horse
  and away he go!
And he never stop at anywhere until he get to Princeton.
And the people, they were just,
  just fixin' up things
    to get ready to move, you know.
But they come.
And the people seen him.
And there were just two rider come.
And when he gets closer
  and one of 'em he said,

    "That was the dead man,
      with 'em.
      He come alive, maybe."

So, when they get there,
  he was alive.
But he awful black on his head, you know.
They really bad.

So the boss, they tell 'em,

    "Well, you lay down and just stay there.
      Till you is better, you know."

But they come alive.
And is after a few days, and they get a little better.
Then they come home.
To Hedley.
That's his home there, in Hedley.
Then he stays home for a while,
  not too long, a couple of weeks,
    and then he rides again
      and he gets better.
See, that's one time he died.

And the second time, died
  right there in Hedley.
About his head too.
That's the same thing, like.
They were threshing the oats in little corral,
  little round corral.
And the horses were just loose in there.
No tie, no halter on 'em—
  just loose.
But somebody on the post near 'em
  and they whip the horses and make 'em run.
And the horses, they fight, you know.
They kick one to another and they fight.
And one of them, they try to jump over the fence,
  at bar end.
Like a bar—that's what—not gate—
  they call 'em a bar.
And they slide them open
  that the horses can get out.
But these horses jump over.
And Charlie's on the other side.
And they run over there to stop the horses
  from jumping.

But anyway, the horses did make a jump.
And then one of these bar,
  they got splintered on the post.
And the post spring out
  and they get hit in the head.
And over they goes.
And they died again.
And the river was just a little ways from there.
That's the Similkameen River.
And they were threshing the wheat
  and Baptiste, he says,

  "Get some canvas for us."

And the boys, you know,
  there were some other boys.

"Get some canvas, a big canvas."

They bring the canvas
  and they put the canvas,
    lay down on the side of Charlie.
Then they roll Charlie on the canvas.
And then they hold the canvas in both end, like.
And then they go to the river
  and then they swing 'em like this,
    two, three times.
Then they throw 'em in the river.
And Charlie, he was floating on the river.
They could see 'em
  and then they don't see 'em no more.

"All right," they said, Baptiste.

"We'll go to the house."

Pretty near noon.
So they walked to the house,
  about a mile, three quarter of a mile.
And only three when they coming.
Supposed to be four,
  but only three,
    when they come.
And they get there.
And they never said nothing.

Baptiste, he says to the boys,

"Don't say anything.
  They can ask, and I can give the answer when they ask,
    but you guys don't say anything."

So, when they get to the house,
  and the womans, they were there, you know,
    they make the dinner ready—
      and they missing one.
And they say,

"Where's the other one?
        Where's Charlie?"

And Baptiste, he says,

"Charlie, he's takin' a bath.
    He's takin' a swim,
        he's takin' a bath,
            he's goin' to swim right down the river
                and then just about there
                    and then he stop
                        and then he come this way.
        By now he's swimmin' there."

He didn't say he died.
So this woman, they just don't know what happened.
It sounds like it seems to be all right,
    but why did he have to swim down the river for?
So after while, in another twenty minutes or so,
    and they see him coming,
        coming out of the river straight from the house.
They walking and walking and he gets there.

See, he's dead, so they threw him in the river.
And he float.
But he come alive while he's on the river, floating.
Then he get out of the river
    and he go to the house.
And that's the second time he died.

And the third time he died,
    he never come alive.
Because the white man trying to handle 'em.
But that time, in the first places, you know,
    in the first two places,
        he use his Indian power.
Then he come alive.
But at the third time,
    the white man tried to handle him.
Well, it's finished.

Run over by a car, him and his horse.
And his horse died and he died.
And they, white people, they think
    maybe they died
        but they think he still breathing . . .
They might take him to hospital
    and maybe after a while they might come to.
So they pick 'em up
    and run 'em to the hospital.
And by the time they get 'em in the hospital,
    little while,
        and then he's dead altogether.

See, that's what happens.
That's three times.
And another time, the same Charlie,
    that was the third time,
        drive the horses,
    the bunch of horses,
        they drive 'em across the river.
At Similkameen River.
And the river was raising already,
    the high water.
Not really high,
    but it's high enough, you know,
        for the horses, they might have to swim.
But they got to take 'em across
    so they could take 'em up on the mountain.
And the other horses, the other people,
    they ride on the horses upstream
        by the church there somewhere.
And then they took the canoe.
And then they went across on the canoe
    so they could have the canoe on the other side.
But these other one, they drive the horses across
    the river, below from the house.
Then they could drive 'em on that side.
When they get there,
    these other boys, they were already waiting there.
And they can get the horses—

they took their horses along with them, you know.
And then they can—
   just so they can get the boat on the other side.
When they come back, they can come across on the boat
   and let the horses swim.
When they come back.

And they drive the horses.
Drive 'em in the river.
And the horse he was riding, that Ya-kum-DI-kin,
   it's not well broke—
      it's kind of half broke
         and it didn't know how to go in the river.
They don't know much about 'em.
And while they in the river, and the other one tell them,

    "Maybe you better carry this gun.
      And I can be headin' off the horses
         without me carrying the gun.
      You take it."

And he give 'em the gun.
Then he had no gun on his hand.
Two rifle.
And his horse, they reared up
   and up and down.
They reared up and then they drop—
   him and the horse and all,
      they sunk in the water.
They watch 'em
   and they don't see him no more.
They roll in the bottom of the river.
But the horses, the bunch of horses,
   they get on the other side
      and the mans, the other mans,
         they get on the other side.
But Ya-kum-DI-kin is disappeared in the water.
They must've flew at the bottom of the river.
And they say a little ways from there,
   was kind of a shallow in the river,

it kind of run a little fast.
And they say they thought they might see the horse.
Might see them when they go over there.
They might stop or else, Ya-kum-DI-kin,
    they might've been drowned too.
And they thought they might get a chance
    to pick 'em up
        and when they get on to the other side
            and they run the horses, two saddle horses,
                and they watch them there.
And not too long, and the horse was rolling,
    then they stop them somehow
        and then they drag 'em out.
Then they take the saddle off, you know.
But the horse is dead.
They drowned.
But where's Charlie?
They don't show up, for little while.
And they was wondering,
    they might've come behind the horse.

But they seen 'em.
Almost in the middle of the river.
And then he come out of the river
    with his head, you know.
And he walk in the bottom of the river
    and then the water going down that way
        because he's walking.
He still have the gun on his hand,
    both of 'em.
When Charlie Allison was telling me that story,
    he's in the bunch when he was a little boy.
And he says they could see 'em,
    they coming out from the river,
        they had the two gun on his hand.
And I says to Charlie, maybe when they dropped
    in the water,
        when he rolled in the bottom of the river,
            and he must've thinking.
He must've thinking this gun worth a lot of money.

I'm not going to let them go.
So they hang on to the gun.
He must've think that.
He must've say that while they were under the water.
He says, maybe could be.

So, they under the water for quite a ways.
Then he come out.
Still have the gun.
He was alive.
But his horse got drowned.
See, that's the third time.
He didn't get killed—
    at the third time, you know.
But nobody can do that.
So that shows he's a power man.
For himself.
But the third time—I mean the fourth time—
    when they run over by car.
And the white people try to handle him,
    then he's dead.
But anyway, he was eighty-one when he died.
That's the fourth time. . . .
See?
All right, that's about all.

PART III

POWER TO DO
THE DOCTORING

GO GET SUSAN, SEE WHAT SHE CAN DO

Susan uses her power to work on two injured men.

There's—a long time ago,
   there one lady down in Omak.
And when she was young,
   that time.
Something like that Napoleon's daughter,
   the one that sing.
About her age.
This woman, they call 'em Susan.
And she go to dance, you know.
Sometimes she put up a dance herself, you know.
In her house.
But sometimes she go to somewhere else, you know.
To somebody's dance.
Like three winter.
She go to a dance.
And sing.
Then, on the third winter,
   she sing in the first winter,
      she never said nothing.
Then she sing, on the second winter,
   for two, three night.
She never said nothing.

But on the third winter,
  she sing for three, four days,
    three, four night,
      and then the dance is finished—
        all over.
Then she say so.
She says,

    "From now on—"

And they stop, you know.
Everybody is just quiet
  and then they talk there.
Just like that—

      Wendy: After midnight?

Well, when they finish,
  before morning . . .
    so that was . . .
They finished then.

      Wendy: Before breakfast?

Before breakfast.
Yeah, when they just finished.
And they know they were finished.
And in morning, you know.
Towards morning.
That was the end.
No more dance after that.
Then is—everybody's quiet.
She must've tell 'em,

    "I'm going to speak.
      And everybody quiet and listen."

Then she stand there
  and she says,

"I'm going to tell you.
  You people . . .
  What I'm going to do.
  From now on.
  I sing three winters,
    and I never said nothing in two winters.
  But this is the third.
  This is the end.
  Now I'm tell you what I'm going to be
    from now on.
  I'm going to be Indian doctor.
  And I'm going to go and work on the sick people.
  Whoever's sick,
    the woman or man,
      or children,
        or any sick person.
  I can go over there if they call me.
  They got to call me.
  Then I can go and work on the sick person.
  And see what I can do.
  Whether I get them to get better,
    or may not.
  Can not tell.

"Then, in another way,
    if somebody gets hurt,
      they got the blood,
        they get hurt,
          then, whoever they get hurt
            then the blood comes inside,
            and they raise up
            that they come to the heart,
            then they's dead.
  And, before the blood comes to the heart,
    and I should suck the blood out.
  And then they never reach the heart.
  And they will get all right.
  They healed up
    and then they'll be all right.

"Or, anybody got the broken leg
   or hurt somewhere,
      maybe no blood in there
         but it more like a—
            kind of a yellow stuff, you know.
They seems to squirt in the inside.
Then that'll come to the heart.
Same as the blood.
But it's yellow stuff.
Something like that over there—yellow.
And they can suck that out.
To keep 'em away from the heart.
And then, once they sucked them out,
   or twice,
      at the same time,
         sucked them out and then stopped
            and then after a little while,
               maybe a few minutes,
                  suck some more.
Then they empty, like.
Then, they never go back.
After a while, whoever they were cut, you know,
   they'll heal up
      and then they's all right."

So he mentioned that he's got two ways.
They can work with the sick people
   or they can work for who they got hurt, you know.
But some doctors, they can only work with the sick people.
Only.
If somebody got hurt,
   they can do nothing for that.
Or somebody got bit with a rattlesnake,
   that's another one.
Somebody's got to do something about it.
But whoever, doesn't matter if it was a doctor,
   Indian doctor,
      but they don't know to fix that rattlesnake bit,
         so they can't do it.
These, the Indian doctor, in another way,

they can work on the sick people.
But the rattlesnake bit,
   they not fit for that.
Some.
But some of 'em, they can do it.
And then some Indian doctor,
   they can be good for the snake bit
     and hurt,
       blood inside,
         and the sick people...
They can be good for three ways.

And, this Susan, she says,

   "This what I'm going to do.
   I'm going to work on the sick people.
   But I got to be called.
   They got to go get me.
   Let me know.
   Then if anybody got hurt,
     as quick as possible,
       let me know to see if I might save 'em."

So, all the people they...
Well, they say,

   "All right.
   We know that."

That's her promise.
Now—that was in the winter,
   about like this.
And, the springtime,
   and about towards the somewhere around the month of June,
     at the same year...
Like, they had that dance
   and she speaks like in the New Year, you know.
After the New Year.
Like in January.
But the next few months,

in June.
And the people were gathered in Omak mission.
To pray.
They call it the Corpus Christi.
The priest, they gathers the people
  and have the big church for two, three days.
And the people come from all over.
From Inchelium, Nespelem,
  and even from Arrow Lake
    and from here,
      from Penticton.
Lot of people.
And they put in the camp along the creek.
And these people,
  they not all good, you know.
Some of 'em bad.
Some of 'em bad people.
But they go over there anyway.
And some of 'em drink, you know.
Then, after they were there,
  about the second night,
    then in the morning,
      just about daybreaks, you know,
        about, four, five o'clock in the morning,
          then one man he was stabbed with a knife in . . .
Right in here.
They cut 'em with a knife.
Then they cut 'em open here.
But, you know, the knife didn't stick right in.
It just kind of cut 'em,
  but it's pretty close to be cut open.
Right inside.
And there's a lot of blood.
Because it open so long, you know.
Then, the people they thought,
  not too long and this man, he'll die.
Because the blood is going to come to his heart.
So some of these older people,
  they said,

"That Susan, they promised to do that kind of way.
    Right now, go get 'em.
    And then, see what they can do."

And she's not there.
She didn't have a camp there
    but she stay home only about six miles.
From mission to Okanogan, Washington,
    here is now, call 'em.
But those days they got a different name, you know,
    in Indian.
And that's where she was.
She tell me that herself.

And whoever they are,
    they go get her
        and they lead the horse.
Because those days, no automobile.
No bicycle, no tractor, no nothing.
Only saddle horse.
And whoever they go get that Indian doctor,
    and that was his brother, the one that got hurt.
And they lead the horse with the saddle on.
So they get her
    to get to her place,
        and they could bring her right away.
Otherwise, if they don't take a horse for her—
    maybe she's got a horse—
        but they might have to hunt for that horse
            and chase 'em around
                and takes a long time to get 'em.
But they lead the horse.
As soon's they get there,
    she can get on that horse
        and they can come.
Then they can work on that man.
So, Susan, she says,
    they were after breakfast
        and they were sitting in the tent

and they had a lot of fun
and play there.
Somebody said to somebody,

"Come down off the hill."

The open side hill.
There's a trail that way,
   but not so steep, you know.
But it's kind of uphill.
She says,

"Somebody come down on that hill.
   They coming pretty fast.
   Running."

So they look for a little while.
They could see they was—
   looked like one man only—
      but they leading a horse.
So, in a little while,
   they come.
Man.
Just one man.
Leading the horse with a saddle on.
Stop.
And then he says to Susan,

"I come and get you.
   My brother, they got hurt.
   Was cut in the side.
   And looks like he's going to die at any time.
   And this is your promise in the powwow time.
   And now that I come and get you,
      it'll be the first time you going to do that.
   You're supposed to do it."

"By God," she says.
"I'm kind of—
   I don't know what to do for a little while."

So, her husband tell 'em,

> "You remember,
> you said that you're going to do it.
> You better go."

So, she says,

> "Just like waking me up."

And then it comes, you know.
His power.
Her power.
All right.

> "All right," they said.
> "I go."

Then they went in the tent.
Then they got some clothes.
They make that dress.
They never wear 'em,
  but only when they can do the doctoring.
Only time that they can wear that certain dress.
Kind of a red.
Then they went over there
  and get that
    and then they take the other one out
      and put that on right away
        and then they get the pipe—
          the smoking pipe.
The stone pipe, you know.
The Indians make them.
About this size.
And this big.
They took that
  and they get some tobacco.
They had that.
They used to be plug, in tobacco.
Just the plug.

More like chewing tobacco.
And they have to cut them with a knife
　　and then smash 'em
　　　　and then put 'em in the pipe
　　　　　　and smoke 'em.
Takes a while to do it.

So they get that.
And then they get on the horse
　　and away they go.
And when they starts from the camp,
　　and it's uphill.
Not steep but it's uphill.
And they kind of a sandy.
A sandy ground.
And the horses,
　　they were galloping up the hill
　　　　on the sandy ground.
Not too long, and they played out.
Then they get to the top
　　and the horses was—
　　　　(makes sound like panting).
You know, they run up the hill.
On—it's kind of sandy.
Then she says to this man who's taking 'em over there,
　　she says,

　　　　"We can turn off the road.
　　　　　　Away from the road.
　　　　　　A little ways.
　　　　　　Then we stop.
　　　　　　And we get off the horses.
　　　　　　I want to smoke."

So they turn off from the road.
And they walk their horses little ways.
Like the road here,
　　and just about like from here to that fence.
Off the road.
And they get off.

And this man, they hold the horses.
Then she sat down and get that tobacco.
And they get the knife and cut 'em.
Cut 'em and finish 'em
    and then they smash 'em.
Put 'em in the pipe.
Light it.
And they smoke.
And that takes a while, you know.
To do it.
Now this man, they thought to himself,

> "By God, I should've have 'em over there.
>   Right away.
>   And they wasting time here.
>   Why do they have to smoke for?
>   He should not smoke.
>   We should not stop here."

He think.
He didn't say,
    but that's in his thought.
Then, when Susan's smoking
    and when he finished smoking
        and he empty the pipe,
            then he says to this man,

> "You were wrong on your thought."

And this man says,

> "Why?"

She says,

> "I will not stop here for nothing.
>   We stop here—
>   I got to smoke to see if I can make it.
>   If I smoke, then I can see that I can never make it—
>   there's no use go,

    because he dead.
But I smoke—
    I got to smoke to see if I can make it.
And then I get there.
As long as I get there,
    they's going to get better.
But now I know.
I can see.
I can get there.
And I'm going to get him to be all right.
That's why I smoke.
But you figure is wrong."

She knew.
She knew that man,
    what they thinks.
See, that's funny
    because you can't tell somebody's thought,
      you know.
But the Indian doctor can do.
So after that, then they get on
    and away they go.

When they get to the place
    and—in the camp, you know.
And this man that they get hurt,
    they pile up the pillows
      and blanket and stuff, you know.

And then, the people,
    they pile up the blankets
      and pillows and stuff, you know.
They put it high.
And then they put this man,
    he set there,
      but it's kind of lay against the pillows,
        so they can be sitting
          because if they were laying
            and the blood is going to come sooner to his heart.
But it's got to be sitting

and kind of lay against the pile.
So the blood'll be slow
   not to get to his heart right away.
That's why they make him set.
But it's kind of lay like this, you know.
In the blanket.
Pile of blanket and pillows.

Then, when they stopped.
A little ways, you know,
   the horses.
And then she get off.
Stop the horse.
Then they get off.
She get off and then they—
   her foot is on the stirrup yet.
One of 'em.
The left.
But the right foot,
   it touch the ground.
Step on the ground.
As soon's they step on the ground,
   it just like some power.
HIT! *(slaps hands)*
Her foot, you know.
Then right up.
And his song, they come out right away.
And they sing loud.
Very loud.
And the good song.
And then, turn around and stand there a while.
And sing loud.
And little while,
   and they walk kind of slow.
Not too fast.
They walk towards that man.

They walked over there
   and then they . . .
Before they get too close,

and stop.
She says,

"That man was laying just about like from here
to that wall.
Laying against the pile of blanket."

Then she stop here.
Stand here.
And she sing her song.
And she put their hands like that.
To see.
To put this power to it, you know.
For a few minutes.
For maybe two, three second.
Then she looked
and a lot of people,
they were right close.
She looked this way
and she see one lady there
and she tell 'em,

"Go get me water.
Right from the creek.
Fresh water.
In little pail or basin."

So this woman grab up the basin.
Then she run to the water.
Down in the creek,
not too far,
but it's like from here to that shed maybe.
Then she run down and get water.
And when she come back and tell her,

"Set it right here."

And she was still that far away from that man.
And this water was set alongside of her.
Then this woman that brings the water,

they set back then.
And down it went
  and went to hand
    and kind of washed her hand
      and she pick up the water.
And who can do that?
But she have the water on her hands like that.
Then she throw to that man.
They hit.
He's hit with the water right in the front of 'em.
Then she sing the song
  and down it went
    and she grab the water
      and like that in her hand.
See the water wouldn't stay there if you do it.
Then she threw that.
Again.
Then they hit the water right here.
The water splash him.
That cool him off right down to his foot,
  you know.
And then, after that,
  sing a while,
    maybe two, three second,
      then she walked
        and walked kind of very slow.
And she get close, you know,
  the man lay against the pile of blanket.
Then she stop some place on this side.

Then she opened his shirt, like, you know.
He opened that,
  just to bare it.
And she put her hand.
But not touching the body over there.
Just about four inch away from it.
And this is about four inch away from her mouth.
Just about like that—
  (makes sucking sound).
She suck the blood.

And they could see this swell up
  when they suck the blood.
Then, turn around and whoever,
  before she do that
    and she tell this woman to hold that basin right here.
The basin,
  she hold the basin with the water.
And she suck the blood
  and she turn
    and she spit in the water.
Just straight blood.
And then they make the water a colour by blood.
But you can never see the blood coming out to her mouth.
And you could never see coming out from that man's body.
See, they suck the blood right in the chest here.

And twice, it's just blood,
  kind of black blood,
    and then they stop.
And then they sing.
And they walked that way.
And walked that way.
And then she put her hand like that
  to that man.
Walked over there
  and come around
    and walked that way.
In about a minute or two,
  then she sucked again.
And then, the third time,
  was just a kind of a yellow.
It looked like blood,
  but it's weak.
They getting kind of yellow.
Then, after a while, again.
But just a very little
  and just a yellow.
They emptied.
No more blood.
But still it was cut open.

And she says that was all right.
That'll do.
She says,

>"I go down to the creek and get medicine.
>   And I get 'em myself
>   and I bring 'em
>   and I fix it myself
>   and I put them on the cut."

So she walked down into the creek
    and they find the willow.
You know, those willows in along the creek,
    the willow brush.
Then they get that cut, you know,
    and then they get that bark.
Get them, and then they scrape the top bark,
    you know.
Scrape that off,
    but only the second bark.
And kind of smash it with the stone.
Hammer, smash it.
And then they put them in the water.
And then they put some warm water on 'em.
And they wet that bark.
It's all smashed.
And then they put 'em in the screened rag,
    like mosquito screen,
        so the stuff they wouldn't slide all over.
Put them in there
    and then they put right on the cut.
Right on the cut
    and then they tie 'em on with some other rag.
She says,

>"You just lay there for a while.
>   You lay there before noon."

That was in the morning when they do that.
Somewhere around about half past eight or nine o'clock

in the morning when they doctor him.
They says,

    "You lay here till near noon.
      Before noon, and then you get up.
      Then you walk around.
      Walk around here a while,
        maybe five minutes.
      Then you lay down again.
      You stay there till the sun goes
        halfways from the noon to the set.
      Somewhere round about three o'clock.
      Then you get up and you walked around
        and you go down the creek.
      Then you drink down in the creek.
      You take the little cup or something
        and then you go down and drink
          right from the creek.
      Then you come back.
      And walk around.
      And then, at night, you can lay down
        in a place where your head can be high.
      And the sun, tomorrow just coming out
        from the mountain.
      Just you could see
        and then you get up and walk around.
      You'll be all right.
      You might be sore, little,
        but you will get good."

So this man do that, you know.
Then, she went home.
Then, this man do that,
  all what she told him.
Because there was some others listen there.
Then, the next day, this man is all right.
He gets better.
And then they take a while, you know.
The next week or so,

to heal up.
And then he's all right.

So that, they do that with—
Suck the blood out.
And another time I watching 'em do that.
I was there.
I seen 'em.
They suck the blood out.
This man was chasing horses in the field.
They got some oats,
   the grain about this high.
All ready to cut.
Then some horses,
   they got in.
A bunch of horses.
Then somebody told 'em,

     "The horses is on your grain,
       on oats field."

They took the saddle horse
   and go over there
     and they chase these horses.
Away from there.
Then come out of the ploughed ground
   and they go in the bushy land, like.
But there was a stump hole.
A stump hole about this deep,
   and big.
Stump, you know, they were burned.
Then they got a hole.
Then this horse, they step in these hole
   and over they goes, you know.
They tumble over.
And they lay on them, you know.
They seems still on the horse
   and then they lay on them
     and they hurt his chest.
They hurt bad.

Then this Indian doctor,
  that Susan,
    they's about two, three miles away from that.
They were visiting there.
But she lives in Okanogan.
But she was visiting with her relatives.
And then this, that man that they got hurt,
  his wife, she get on the horse
    and went down to get Susan.
Then they talk to Susan.
When we seen 'em,
  the two of us.
And they bring 'em.
Susan come and they's going to ride a horse . . .
From their people, who they're visiting.
They got a horse.
They could ride that horse
  and then come.
And myself and another boy,
  we work at the barn, you know,
    fixing the barn.
Fixing the stall, you know,
  so we can put some horses in.
Then they stop and then they tell us,
  they tell us,

    "You.
      You boys should come with me.
      You could, after a while.
      I'm going to fix that man that got hurt.
      But I want you boys to come.
      I need the help."

    "All right."

I said,

    "We'll go after a while.
      In little while.
      Another half hour or so and I will go."

It was in towards evening, like.
So they left,
   and after a little while,
      about half an hour,
         or three quarter hour after that,
            then we come.

Then we come to the place
   and it's getting to be about supper time.
And then she says,
   when we get there,
      and they says to us,

      "You boys just stay here.
         I'm not going to do any work till it gets dark."

So it's just like about nine or ten o'clock.
That was in the summer, you know.

      "I'm not going to do the work till it gets dark.
         This man is all right.
         They'll be all right.
         I'm not going to do any work till it gets dark.
         But I want you to be here."

And I don't know what did they want us for.
So we stay there.
And there was not only that man and his wife
   but there was some others, you know.
And they cooking
   and they give us eating.
But the Indian doctor, they don't eat.

So we waited.
In the summer, till it gets dark,
   about ten o'clock.
Maybe half past nine,
   it's getting to be dark.
Now, he said,

"All right.
I'm going to work on him."

So this man was laying on the bed like that.
But they make a high pillow.
Pile up the quilts and pillow,
and they just lay high, you know,
his head high.
They were over there.
And he tell me,
he says,
that doctor, he says,

"You stand over there.
Just like over there, like."

Because the bed was right at the wall.
Right in the corner.
He says,

"You stand over there."

And the other boy, he's younger than me,
he says,
she says to him,

"You stand here."

They put us—me—way over there,
and the other boy here.
But the other people they was still sitting.
Then she was standing alongside of that man
and she sing her song
and sing her song.
And she says,

"I'm going to suck this stuff out.
They's might've be a little blood,
not too much."

She says to me,

"You come and open the shirt."

So I unbuttoned the shirt
  and then open 'em this way.
And I went back.
And that's all I do.
She says,

"I need the help."

Oh, she could do that.
They want me to do it.
And this other boy,
  they just want 'em to stand there.
To see.
So, I seen 'em.
I watch 'em.
Because, it's, you know, just like from here to there.
And I watch them
  and she come here to put her hand like that.
And then she had the water.
All ready.
Oh yes, this boy was holding this water.
My friend.
He holding that basin.
But I didn't hold nothing,
  but I open the shirt for that man.
Then I stand right close.
Walks there and puts her hand like that—
  I could seen 'em.
They leave it open like that, you know.
Not tight, it just kind of open.
And then they put it.
It was about, I can tell,
  about four inch away from the chest.
And then about four inch away from her mouth.
They seem to do like that—

(makes sucking sound).
But this is far, far away from her mouth.
And far away from the body.
Then they—
   (makes sucking sound again).
Then I could see this blew up.
Then they turned around
   and this boy, they put that water to it, you know.
And she spit, kind of mixed with blood.
Kind of yellow stuff and blood.
And she sing and she dance around there.
She just dance.
Just back and forth.
Dance and dance
   and she picks up
      and in a few minutes
         and she sucked again.
But just yellow stuff.
Then, after a little while,
   about five, ten minutes,
      then she sucked again.
Just a little bit,
   just a yellow.
That's all.
That'll never go back.
Once she suck 'em,
   then that's finished.
Then, she says,

   "You just lay there.
      Tomorrow, soon's the sun comes out of the mountain,
      sun raised,
         just so's you can see the sun,
            then you get up.
      And then you walk around.
      And you go to the creek
         and then you get there.
      It's not good for you to lay there and drink,
         but take a cup
            and get the water and drink.

And then you can walk around.
Two, three days . . .
You'll be all right."

So, they all right.
In a few days, I seen 'em again.
He's all right.

So, this last stories.
This I was telling you—
  that I seen 'em.
I was there.
Now the other stories, that one,
  the fellow was cut,
    that she tell me herself.
All about.
So I really know.
That's the way I seen.

SING YOUR SONG
AND TAKE THE
SICKNESS AWAY

A man is upset when he hears that his cousin is critically ill. In a dream, his power instructs him to go and visit the sick man.

This another one, it's very clear.
A man, he lives across the river from Cawston.
His name John.
John Kwee-LA-kin.
And the other guy, they lived on the bench.
On the Cawston Bench,
    up to the creek there.
See, that just about two miles
    apart, where they lived.
They are cousins.
But John Kwee-LA-kin, he got a job working
    on the pack train from Hope to Princeton.
And he goes over there and works for Allison.
Allison is the boss.
He runs the pack train.
But he got to hire some people, you know.
White people, or Indian.
Mostly Indian.
Those days, a lot of Indian.
Not so many white people.
Those days.

That back in sixties and seventies.
Long time ago.
1860s and 1870s, along that time.

And this other one, he lives at the Cawston Bench.
His name Paul.
Paul Terbasket.
And John Kwee-LA-kin, he lives across the river.
He heard that Paul was kind of sick.
He was sick.
Not too bad, but he's not working.
He's sick.
And they go to work for the pack train.
They worked there about two months.
Maybe three month.
All summer.
And every time he come back from Hope
    and he heard about 'em.
Somebody sent a word.
Because from here they go to Princeton.
For supply, you know.
And they, Allison is the boss, like,
    run everything, you know.
And they find that out from the people
    that Paul Terbasket was still sick.
They getting worse.

Every time John Kwee-LA-kin come back from Hope,
    like every two weeks or so,
        and they heard about 'em.
They getting bad.
They getting worse.
But, that last time, when they leave back to Hope,
    and the boss told 'em,

    "This time, this is the last trip.
        You go down, you guys, and bring the stuff.
        And get back.
        And no more work for a while.

You can go home for two weeks, three weeks.
Then you come back and are back again
    till the snowfall.
And it gets to be winter.
But now we're going to stop for about three weeks.
Lay off."

So, he know that.
But he went back to Hope to get one more trip.
And he get the stuff.
Not only him, but bunch of 'em.
They bring the stuff and they get back to Princeton.
Late that night, the evening.
They kind of tired.
They ride it all day to Princeton.
They supposed to go home, but next day.
They got to stop.
They got to have the rest for that night.
The next day they can go home.
And, soon as they come back
    and they heard that Terbasket is getting lower and low.
It looks like he's going to die.
By God, he thought, that was his cousin.

He thought,

    "By God, I'll be lucky if I see him again.
        What I heard, he just about dying now.
        But I can't go tonight.
        I'm too tired.
        In the morning I'll go home.
        I might see 'em."

That's what he think.
So that night, they stopped there and go to bed, asleep.

When he was a-sleeping
    and his power told him,

        "John, look at that man."

He take a look,
   from Princeton to Cawston Bench.
But he can see.
See that man.
And they looked at 'em
   and that was Paul.
He looked pretty bad.
And his power told 'em,

   "Now. Tomorrow.
      You go home, and not to go to see 'em.
      Keep on goin' and you get home.
      And you stay overnight at your home.
      When the sun goes down, you make a KWEELSH-tin,
         sweathouse.
      You make a sweathouse
         and you go in the sweathouse four times.
      Then you quit for that night.
      The next morning, early in the morning,
         you make another sweathouse.
      You go in four times.
      Before the sun comes up.
      You quit sweathouse before the sun comes up.
      But don't eat.
      Don't eat breakfast.
      Don't eat nothing in the morning.
      You wait till the sun comes up,
         and he come up a little higher.
      Take your horse and you go to Paul Terbasket.
      When you get there, there's a lot of people there.
      Lot of Indians.
      When you get there,
         they could see you coming.
      And they could see that John Kwee-LA-kin,
         they come.
      Maybe they come to see his cousin.
      And when you get close, they might say,

         'Hello, John.'

They talk to you.
Don't pay no attention to anybody.
Don't talk to nobody.
Never mind.
Doesn't matter if they talk to you.
Keep going.
Keep walking.
Tie your horse and keep walking.
Don't look at nobody.
Don't say nothing to anybody.

And then you come to where Paul was.
And you just get there
    and stand and sing this song.
You sing the song and you chuck it up in your hands.
In little while, you can ask any of them,
    somebody will be setting there,
        to get you water.
And they can bring the water in little pail.
And wash your hand
    and throw the water in their head.
Then you sing your song and you fix 'em up
    and you take the sickness away from them.
Then wouldn't be long,
    they'll be all right.
That day, the next day,
    if they want to eat something,
        they could give 'em what they want to eat.
And they get all right."

See? His power told 'em all about what he's going to do.
When he wake up, was still in Princeton.
But, after breakfast, about nine o'clock,
    and then he started to come home.
And they go by Keremeos and they kept a-going.
He don't go to Paul's place.
He keep a-going and go across and get home.
Kind of early.
About four o'clock in the afternoon.
And he get home.

After a little while,
   he went and fix up the sweathouse.
And just as soon as the sun goes down,
   then they burn.
Then put the stone in the sweathouse
   and he go in the sweathouse four times.
And he go back to the house
   and his wife and then his mother
     she already cooking, you know.
And he going to eat.
And his wife told 'em,

    "Well, John, you comin'.
      We going to help you."

He said,
    "No.
      You people eat that.
      I'm not going to eat."

    "Why?"

    "Oh, I don't feel like eatin'.
      I'm not goin' to eat.
      Maybe after a while."

That's what he says.
So finally she, this young lady, John's mother,
   she told 'em,

    "Never mind.
      If he say that, he might know what he's doing."

So they leave 'em alone.
And these other people eat
   but he didn't eat.
And, after the sweathouse.
After a while, kind of late,
   and he go to bed.

He go bed.
Before they go to bed and he says to his wife,

> "We don't have to lay together.
>   We don't have to sleep together.
>   You make a bed over there somewhere.
>   And you sleep there by yourself.
>   I want to lay here by myself, alone.
>   For the night."

And the old lady says,

> "Why?"

You know, his wife.

> "Ah," he says,
> "Never mind.
>   Make up your bed and I'll sleep here alone."

So they do.
Next morning, early, he get up
    and make a sweathouse
        and they burn 'em
            and he go to sweathouse.
And before the sun comes up.
And then he come back.
And the same way.
They already cook.
They going to eat.
And told 'em,

> "You going to eat?"

He says,
> "No.
>   I'm not goin' to eat."

But in the evening, he don't eat at the supper time
    but late.

He eat little bit.
Not much.
In morning, he never eat breakfast.
And they said,

> "After while, when the sun comes up,
>   I got to go and see my friend.
>   See how he get along."

So, wait for the sun.
Till the sun comes up.
He saddle his horse and he go.
They not far, only two miles.
They get there and then they all open, you know.
No orchard those days.
Just the sagebrush and the bunch grass.
And they could see them comin'.
So they know.
The people know John is coming home.
He come back.
He say,

> "That John is coming.
>   He coming to see his friend, I guess."

Then everybody watching him.
And he stop and tie up his horse
    and then he come.
And some of them said,

> "Hello, John.
>   Finally you got here."

Never look.
He don't pay no attention.
They just keep walking,
    till he come to where Paul was,
        in the tent, you know.
He stand there.
They lay, you know, in the tent.

They stand from over there, by their feet.
Started to sing his song.
Loud.
Right away loud.
Sing his song for a few minutes.
Two minutes, maybe.
Then he says to lady,

    "Get me water."

So this lady, she jump.
And she went to the creek and says,

    "Get me fresh water."

And they get them from the creek,
   in the basin or something.
Put it there and he washed his hand.
And he worked on the sick man.
Then he sing his song.
And everybody stop and just watching him.
They don't talk to 'em any more.

He worked there for a while.
And then he stopped.
He finished.
And he says to these other people,

    "Whenever Paul—maybe today sometimes—
      maybe in the afternoon.
    If he says he was hungry,
      ask him what he wants.
    What he should eat.
    He could say.
    He might mention or something.
    Whatever they want to eat,
      give 'em that.
    If you didn't have 'em, go and look for it
      as quick as you can get 'em."

That's what he says.
Well he knows but he wouldn't tell all.
So he says,

> "That's what I'm goin' to tell you.
>   And now I go home."

That's all.
He don't stay there and talk to the people.
Just tell that and go back,
   get on the horse
      and go home.

So that day, they watching him.
They watchin' him till the sun pass noon.
About two, three o'clock.
And then he moved around, and he said,

> "Is somebody here?"

> "Yes."

His mother there.
Then his wife.
And some others.

> "Yeah. We're all here."

Says,

> "By God, I was hungry."

He said,

> "Yeah, you're hungry."

He says,

> "Yeah, really hungry."

"What do you think you should eat?
What did you wish to eat?"

"Well, by God, it's hard to get,
but I'd like to eat fish."

Well, there is no fish there.
Fish is down the creek,
down the river.
There was fish there,
but not there at the camp.
So these ladies, right away they talk to one another
and there was quite a bunch of boys around.
They says to the boys,

"Come here."

And the boys go over there.
And tell 'em, the boys, the two, three of 'em,
and tell 'em,

"You and you and there.
Three of you.
Go out and get some grasshopper right away.
Get it two, three.
And get some horses and go down the river.
Run! Just run and get the river.
And each one can fish.
And the other one over there.
And the other one there.
And the other one farther down.
So whoever get one, only one fish,
come back right away.
Because we need that.
That sick man, he want to eat fish."

So the boys, because they knew that work,
they got to ask for something to eat.
The boys, they run out and get some grasshopper.
They might've get one or two, you know.

And the other one the same.
Then they get the fishhooks
   and get on the horse
      and AWAY they go to the river.
They run all the way till they get to the river.
Put 'em on the stick and then they fished there.
And then the other one over there.
In little while, one of 'em, they got one.
Not pretty big.
And he says,

   "I got one.
      All right. Let's go back."

Only one.
They run back.
That was a trout they get.
When they get back to the camp
   and give 'em to the ladies
      and these ladies they already boil the water
         there over the open fire.
And they cooked them right away.
And they watched 'em till they was cooked
   and they put 'em away till they cool off.
And told him,

   "Here's the fish.
      You eat that.
      You want the soup?"

He said,

   "Yes."

And they eat just a little.
Just maybe half a swallow.
Just very little.
And then he take a drink in the spoon.
Just about half a spoon,
   the soup, fish soup.

Drink that.
He said,

    "That's enough.
       That's good."

And he don't eat till night.
The next morning, as soon as the sun was up,
   he's hungry again.
Because they have that fish there.
And then he eat again.
They keep doing that, pretty soon he eat a little more.
And he eat that fish maybe five, six days.
And he eat 'em all.
Only one fish.
Take him about five, six days to finish 'em.
Eat 'em.

And then he get better.
Pretty soon he be all right again.
And John Kwee-LA-kin he died first.
Before Paul.
See, that's the way, you know.
That's the Indian way.
But some of them, they was never told by his power.
Whoever was sick, maybe his mother or his wife,
   they can go and see the Indian doctor.
And ask 'em to come to work for 'em.
That's another way they do.
But in another way, that's the first time
   that John Kwee-LA-kin do that kind of work.
And then they do that kind of work since.
For a while, but they quit.
Quit altogether.
He don't do that no more.

See?
That's the way they do.

GRAB THE SICKNESS
AND SEND 'EM OUT

Charlie Stewart, an Indian doctor in Merritt, has a vivid dream in which he is summoned to Hedley to attend to a very sick man.

Charlie Stewart, he's an Indian doctor.
He works for the sick people.
He's a real Indian doctor.
Everybody know.
And he lives in Merritt.
And there's a fella here.
He lives here, right here by the church.
That's Hedley Indian church.
He live there.
That's Carrie's stepfather.
His name Dan Tooma.
That was his name, that man.
He lives there.
And Carrie's mother were married to Dan Tooma.
So they lived there.
They had the family.
Carrie was in the bunch,
    but they were just a small.
At that time, that's quite a few years ago.
But at the time, Carrie was just about
    maybe three, four years old.
At that time.
And that Dan Tooma, he got sick.
He was sick and sick and sick.

They give 'em medicine.
They don't go to a doctor those days.
The Indian.
Not like today.
The Indian they was sick,
   is sick at home.
Maybe the Indian doctor can work on 'em
   or maybe some of his people,
     if they know some medicine,
       then they can work on 'em.
But they don't go to hospital.
They don't go to white man doctor.
Those days.
So this Dan Tooma was sick.
Sick for quite a while.
He been sick for about two months.
At home.
He all right.
He can get up and go outside.
Those days no toilet in the house.
Not like today.
They got to go out.
The toilet is in outside.
And he can get up and go to toilet.
And come back.
He might set round at the table
   and eat very little.
And then he go back to bed.

But, he keep getting lower and lower.
And lower and lower and lower.
And the priest,
   because that was the church,
     the priest comes there once in a while.
And the priest goes over there
   and then pray for Tooma, for Dan Tooma.
Pray and bless him
   and give 'em Holy Communion
     and go to confession and so on.
Ready to die.

But don't do anything to either way.
He don't die
    but they don't get better.
Been that way long time.

And the people talked about, you know.
They, all over,
    they heard that in Merritt.
Some people, Indian people in Merritt,
    they heard Dan Tooma was pretty sick.
Been sick quite a while.
Still sick.
He getting worse.
He getting lower and lower.
Looks like he's going to die.
They talked about it.
And Charlie Stewart, he's an Indian doctor.
He heard that.
He heard the people talked about.
But only, he heard, you know.

And he thinks about it.
One night, he thinks about it.
By God, that man is not old.
He just a middle-aged man.
Too bad he was sick.
Kind of think about it.
Then he went to sleep.
While he was sleeping
    and his power,
        could be his bird or animal,
            his power anyway.
They come to him.
When he was sleeping.
That's his dream.
And told 'em.
And told 'em,

        "Stewart. Stewart.
            Look at that man."

And Stewart, they look from Merritt to Hedley.
And they can see that far.
See to Dan Tooma.
They see 'em.
He look pretty bad.
And whatever they were talking to 'em
    and told 'em,

     "You see that man.
       He's going to die
         and not too long from now.
       They gettin' lower and lower.
       Tomorrow, you go.
       Tomorrow night you get there.
       Tomorrow night.
       You get there just when it get dark.
       Just about gettin' dark
         and then you get there.
       Then, you go in the house.
       Don't talk to nobody.
       Just go in the house
         and you could see him where he lay
           in the house."

There is no kitchen.
There's just one room, you know.
There was a kitchen in one end
    and a bed in one end.

     "As soon as you go in you could see him.
       And just walk up to him.
       And stand alongside of him
         and sing this song.
       Then you sing the song a while
         and then you tell somebody to get you water.
       Then when you get the water,
         you work on him that night,
           as soon's you get there.
       And you stay there for overnight.

Next morning the sun comes up
    and you work again on him for a little while.
And the same day you can come back
    if you wanted.

"And after that, they wanted to eat for some kind.
    Anything they want to eat,
        they can eat.

"They don't tell 'em what to eat
    but they tell me they get hungry,
        then they eat.
They keep eating little more.
And little more
    and little more
        and they get better,
           get better,
             get better.
Wouldn't be long and then
    they'll be all right again.
You have to do it."

His, his power told him.
Well, he got to do it.
If he don't, it liable to be bad for him.
So he got no money.
He got money,
    but not enough.
And he got to make it that day.
He got to come on the bus.
At that time the bus comes from Kamloops
    and stop in Merritt
        and then come from Merritt to Princeton.
And then back.
So he got to catch that.
And he got to get to Princeton.
And then they supposed to be another bus goes by there.
And it goes right over to Hope.
So they can catch that.

By God, the next morning he had to go out
  and rustle for some more money.
And finally he get it.
He get money.
He get enough money to come on the bus and back.
So he wait for the time,
  till the time comes,
    about—somewhere around after two o'clock.
Because he get off here
  about five o'clock in the evening.
Maybe six, something like that.
From there.
Those days, the bus,
  they got different times going through here.
So he catch the bus from Merritt
  and then he come to Princeton
    and then he get to Princeton.
He wait a while
  and then the other bus comes through from Hope.
That's from Vancouver, like,
  you know, come through that.
And they catch that bus.
Then they get up there.
About six, or maybe after six.

And because Holmes was saying
  his wife was washing dishes after supper
    and then they finished.
Just about finished.
And they could hear.
They little ways,
  the house just little ways from their house.
They could hear somebody sing,
  or something.
Because the house is open.
Is not cold.
That was in the month of September.
And the house is open.
And when Stewart gets off from the bus,
  it getting dark, you know.

Just about getting dark.
And he walk to the house.
He get off at the road
    and then he walk to the house.
And he, he knocked on the door.
Someone open the door
    and they go in
        and try to say hello—
            he don't pay no attention.
He walk to that sick man
    and he stand alongside of him
        and he started to sing his song.
And the people, they stop.
And they just let him do it.

Sing his song
    and a little while he says to Dan's wife,

    "Get me some water in the basin."

And she get up and get him some water
    and then he wash his hands.
Work on that sick man.
Sing the song.
Loud.
And he dance,
    himself only.
But the others, they just sittin' there.
He work there for a little while.
And he stopped.
And then he says,

    "That's enough for now.
        Tomorrow morning, the sun comes up,
            I work again for a little while.
            Then I go home."

So, they go to sleep.
They all go to bed.
Tomorrow morning when the sun up,

not too high,
    as soon's they come up a little ways,
      and he go to work again the same way.
He sing the song
  and dance
    and he use his hands, you know,
      to grab the sickness.
Send 'em out in the air.
He finish.

Then, he said,

    "I want to catch the bus.
      I want to get."

He figure out, there is no bus to catch,
  to make the right time to Princeton.
So finally someone,
  I think Charlie Allison or somebody,
    they got the car,
      or Harry Skwakin maybe.
They took 'em in the car to Princeton.
And then he catch the bus from Princeton.
To Merritt.
He get home.

But Dan Tooma, that day when the sun is way down,
  and he said,

    "I'm hungry."

They ask him,

    "What do you want?"

    "Oh well, maybe make kind of a flour.
      Make a little flour, mix 'em
        with the grease, lard or something.
      Make kind of a soup,
        but mostly flour."

Just like you making hotcakes, you know.
And they cook that.
And he drink that.
Next morning he eat again.
He getting up.
He getting up,
    he getting better.
Fast.
In a couple of weeks
    then he walks around.
He's all right.
He getting better in about a month.
He's okay.
He ride a horse and go someplace
    just like anybody.
And he was alive a long time after.

And old Stewart, he died.
But Dan is still alive.
But he died about three years ago,
    four years ago.
He died in the second of February,
    in the Groundhog Day.
He died in Penticton Hospital.
So that's that for that Indian doctor.
Charlie Stewart.
He was told by his power to do that.
And he did do it.
And he get the man better.
So that's all.
That's short, that story.

DON'T FORGET
MY SONG

When Harry's life is threatened on two occasions, an Indian doctor inter-venes.

Yeah, this one time—
   Awk-MEEN—that was her Indian name.
But her gaved name was Margaret.
She's a Indian doctor.

Yeah.
And one time, that we're together . . .
Her—and I got a woman that time.
Not my wife, but that was the first one I had,
   but we're not married.
But we're together for a while, you know.
Two, three months.
Four months.
And then, in the fall,
   in the month of September,
      and Awk-MEEN told us maybe we should go down to Omak.
And see if we can get a job picking apples.
Now is the time to pick apples.
We can all go.
And we can be together.
We can find a cabin
   and we can live there together.
Helping one another
   because she's all alone.

She don't like to be living there some place alone.
But when you—us—
    and her—
        then it will be three of us.
That's what she want.
And we agree that way
    because she know the places . . .
They used to work there.
So we went.
She got a buggy and they got one horse—
    the one-horse buggy.
And I got a saddle horse.
Then when we moved,
    when we go to Omak from Chopaka,
        and I and my woman, we were sitting,
        and we drive the horse, you know,
            in the buggy.
But she riding my saddle horse.
And then they ride behind us.
And then we go on the road.
In those days, no car, you know.

So we get to Omak.
This side of Omak,
    they call 'em Riverside.
I told you when we go by there
    that this is Riverside.
The old road . . .
No road that way at that time.
But that was the old road.
It goes up the hill a bit.
When we get up to the top of the hill
    and it was a farm up there.
They got some apples.
And she said to us,

    "This place, I work to this place at one time.
        Maybe we stop
            and you can go and ask 'em if they need somebody
                for picking apples."

And, she says,

> "You mention my name.
> That he knows me.
> They might give us a job."

All right.
We stopped on the road
  and I just walk from the road to the house.
And, a white man come out
  and I says, I mention her name.
I says that,

> "That was the lady that you must've known.
> She says she know you.
> And we are—"

I said,

> "We are looking for jobs,
>   picking apples."

And he asked us how many of us.

> "There just the three of us,
>   and we got two horses."

Says,

> "That'll be fine.
> That'll be good.
> I only need about three.
> That's all."

He says,

> "You fellas can work."

He says,

"This is the cabin there.
   And then they could stay in there.
   There's a lot of wood.
   I can bring some wood
      and then you can use wood for cooking."

Because, those days, no electricity,
   no stove like that.
It was just wood.
All right, we get a job.

And then, we stay there.
And the cabin was two room.
In one room, that's where they cook
   and that's where the stove was.
And we cook there.
And this lady, she sleeps in the same room.
But there was another room.
That was supposed to be the bedroom.
But just small.
And I and my woman,
   we sleep over there in the room.
But she sleeps in the kitchen.
For a few days we work there.
And we were together.
So, she works alone.
She pick apples alone.
Herself.
That's for her, you know.
But I and my woman, we picked together.
Mix 'em, you know.
That's our work.
Two, three night.
Maybe more—one week, I think.
And one night, after supper,
   and we sitting there and talk stories,
      after a while,
         and then we go to bed.
And she had the bed in the kitchen.

And about, could be around one o'clock in the morning,
   and I heard 'em singing.
In the dark, you know.
Because we shut the light off.
She was singing.
Sing her Indian doctor song.
And I woke up.
She was singing.
And I just listen.
After a little while—
   she was singing for about five, ten minutes—
      then she says,

     "Did you guys awake?"

I said,

     "Yeah. I wake up.
       And my woman, she wake up too."

And she says to us,

     "You better get up and dress up
        and come in here.
      And put the light on.
      And then I can sing
        and they can help me sing.
      And we can all sing together."

Well, she's Indian doctor, you know.
We've got to do what she says.
So we get up and dress up
   and we go in to light the lamp.
It's not like this,
   the lamp, you know.
Coal oil.
We light that.
Then she was sleeping with the mattress
   just on the floor,

and she get up
    and she sat there.
And we sat close to her.
She sing her song
  and we sing too.
The same song.
We all sing together.
Only one song though.
For a while.
Then she stop singing.
Then she says to me,

> "There was something under your pillow.
>   Your pillow.
>   There was something under your pillow.
>   I want you to go get 'em.
>   And give it to me."

Well, I knew there was something under my pillow.
It was a pistol.
A little.32 revolver.
So, she mentioned that.
They didn't say,

> "You got a gun there."

But she says,

> "There was something under your pillow.
>   I want you to go get 'em
>   and give it to me."

So I know what was under my pillow.
And I went and get 'em.
And, I give it to 'em.
But she says,

> "Lay it down there."

And I laid 'em down.
On the front of her.
And she sing the song, for a while.
They sing the song.
Then they grab the gun.
They looked at 'em
   and they turn 'em over
      and looked.
Then they put it down.
Then, she says to me,

   "This is not good.
      This, this gun here,
         this is the one they going to kill you.
      That's what I see in my dream.
      But now that I'm going to fix 'em up,
         and I'm going to do what I can,
            so all this what I say in the bad trick,
               the bad way,
                  I'm going to take 'em away.
      So they wouldn't be here.
      But we got to have something for help.
      You have to watch that till morning."

She says,

   "There is someone is going to get you.
      Then he's going to take this gun
         and he going to kill you with that gun.
      It was your gun,
         but whoever they are,
            they're going to use your gun to kill you.
      But we'll see what we can do."

So they sing awhile
   and she got the hair—
      but the hair was braided, you know.
Long hair.
And she says to this woman,

"You undo this braid here,
    and you let my hair loose,
        but tie 'em here with a little string."

And they let the hair go down on her back.
So she told them that.

"I'll braid this
    and then to keep them together
        and tie 'em here."

And they just hanging this way.
A long hair—right down.
Then they sing again.
Sing again for a while.
They be singing there for about an hour—
   maybe more.
She says,

    "That'll be enough for tonight.
      We can go to bed again."

    "But," she says.
    "Early in the morning—"

I usually get up early anyway
   because we're working.
I get up about five o'clock.
Half past four.
Just as soon's it get daylight
   and then we go to pick apples.
I get up every morning—early.
She says,

    "When you get up in the morning—
      early—
        you build a fire
           and put some hot water.
   Make hot water.

When you finished building the fire,
   you go outside.
And look around.
You look at the sky.
See what you can see on the sky.
If there's any blue only.
Or cloud.
You might see some cloud.
Or may not.
Maybe nothing but blue sky."

So, we go to bed.
Go to sleep.
But early in the morning, I get up.
I went to build a fire.
After I build 'em,
   I put some water on the stove,
     for coffee.
I went outside.
Then I went down and I look around.
Could never see no cloud anywhere.
Not a little one.
They just nothing but blue.
Blue cloud.
So I come in.
And I says to her,
   there nothing I seen.
Nothing but blue cloud.
She says,

   "All right.
     Maybe after a while we might—
       you might see some cloud
         and you might see clouds there—
           very small.
     Some place.
     After a while, in another half hour or so,
       you take another look."

So, we wait a while.
Then they get up.
And they cook breakfast.
And, a little while,
   about half an hour,
      and she tell me,

      "You go out.
         Look at the sky."

I went out and looked the same.
Nothing.
No cloud.
Nothing.
I come in and I said,

      "There is no cloud or nothing."

      "All right," she says.
      "After a while, in another half hour,
            you go out again.
         See if you could see some cloud.
         You might see."

In another half hour, I went out.
It was the same thing.
Three times, no cloud.
No nothing.
So, when I go in and we eat,
   we eat breakfast then.

Then I went out.
Then I see the sky.
I mean the cloud.
The mountain is like that—
   ridge that way—
      and this is ridge.
And that's where I see the cloud,

right in between these mountain like that.
They just a very little.
Just a little bit,
    just enough to see.
But the rest of 'em all blue.
I come in and I says,

    "I did see a cloud,
        but very small.
      Right in the west.
      Right where that mountain goes like that."

She says that sign is good.
She says,

    "That's going to get bigger.
      After a while.
      Keep coming.
      That cloud is coming from the west.
      Right from the sea.
      It's coming.

    "After a little while,
        we could see 'em bigger.
      Then if it gets to be bigger
        and it keeps a-coming
          and it kept a-coming
            and pretty soon and it'll be all cloud.
      Be black cloud.
      And then the cloud is going to go to the east.
      And then, another thing,
        we have to watch the sun.
      And the sun is going to come out from the mountain
        on the east.
      It going to come out.

    "We can see them coming out.
      Just see them.
      And then the cloud is going to cover 'em.

And we don't see 'em no more.
But they come out of the mountain already.
And then a little while after that,
　　the rain is going to come down.
Going to be a heavy rain.
Just pour.
That's what we're going to see.
You just watch.
You take a look every once in a while."

Well, I don't know.
I thought, I don't know.
Might be—not.

In a little while, they always there.
Go out and look.
And I went out
　　and this cloud was getting bigger.
I come in and I says,

　　"That cloud is getting bigger
　　　　and it was kind of black too."

All right.

Pretty soon I go out again.
That's pretty fast,
　　and it was pretty high.
Almost above us already.
I come in and I tell 'em,
　　and she says that was all right.

　　"Next, we got to watch the sun."

So next time I went out
　　and then the cloud was past us
　　　　and it was quite a ways—
　　　　　　that ways, to the east, already.
And I said to her,

"The cloud is passing us.
     But it's still a long ways to go yet."

She says,

"That's all right.
     You got to watch the sun.
     The sun comes out from the mountain
          just enough to see.
     Then the cloud could cover 'em.
     And that'll be really good.
     But if they don't—
          not so good.
     So, in a little while,
          not too long,
               take a look."

And I take a look
     and then the cloud was getting close to the mountain.
In the east.
But the sun is bright already.
Not coming out yet
     but you could see it brighten already.
Then we just sit there and watch 'em.
And a little while and we see the sun
     just ways come out from the mountain.
The whole sun—
     we seen 'em.
And then that cloud,
     it just cover 'em.
That's the way.
See, everything they says,
     it comes right.

And then, she says,

"In little while, maybe ten minutes,
     maybe a little more,
          the rain is going to come.
     It going to be a heavy rain."

So we sat down in the house.
In a little while, about seven minutes,
    something like that,
        and then we can hear the roof.
Just like if you pour the big pail of water on the roof
    you could hear them.
The rain was just down.
For a little while.
Rained about an hour—heavy.
And then they quit.
Quit raining.
And then the sun was—
    we didn't see the sun again,
        still cloudy,
            but we knew the sun was quite a ways up.
She says,

        "All right.
            We sit down and we sing again.
            Just like we do last night."

So we sit down on her bed.
And then we all sing.
And they had that gun—
    when I give it to 'em—
        and they had them
            and then she says,

        "We going to bed,
                I put this gun under my pillow.
            And I'm going to keep it under my pillow.
            Instead of you taking 'em back."

So they take that gun
    and put 'em under her pillow.
And it was there yet
    when she sing last time.

And then, when they singed at the second time,
    after breakfast,

we sing together for a while,
　　and we stop
　　　　and they take that gun
　　　　　　and take a look
　　　　　　　　and looked at 'em.
And she says,

　　"I put them back under my pillow.
　　　　Maybe I keep 'em there for the day."

She says,

　　"After a while, before noon,
　　　　they going to clear up
　　　　　　and they going to dry up
　　　　　　　　and then you guys can go out
　　　　　　　　　　and pick if you want to.
　　But I want to get on the saddle horse
　　and I want to go to Omak."

It's only about two, three miles from there to Omak.
Then they said,

　　"I'm going to spend the all day today."

That was Saturday.

　　"And then, I'm going to spend tomorrow there.
　　　　But tomorrow night, on Sunday night,
　　　　　　kind of early,
　　　　　　　　maybe five o'clock,
　　　　　　　　　　and I'll come back."

And she says, everything is all right.
Not to worry anything.
What I tell you, they all the same.
Her word is always true.
Whatever she says, is like that.
But she says,

"Somebody is going to have a blood.
　Maybe today,
　　maybe tomorrow.
　But somebody's going to get hurt.
　And they's going to be bleeding.
　Not here.
　It's going to be somewhere else.
　But in the first place,
　　that blood's supposed to be here.
　I take 'em away.
　Now we're okay.
　You don't have to worry for anything.
　But I have to watch you here.
　Somebody'll be hurt.
　Maybe today, maybe tomorrow."

So they went.
I take the horse and saddle 'em
　and she ride and go to Omak.
So, after a while we were still in the house,
　it's about eleven o'clock,
　　and I look.
By gosh, it's dry there.
Quit raining and wind blows a little
　and the trees were dry.
So we go out and pick.
Pick apples all day.

She never come back that night.
She was at the Omak.
Sunday morning,
　about nine o'clock in the morning on Sunday—
　　see this was a Saturday morning when we sing.
When we got that rain,
　on Saturday morning.
But it clear up and it's all right again
　before noon.
The same day.
She went to Omak.

And they stay there all day.
And they stay there all night.
For stick game, you know.
Some people, they play stick game
  and some people go to work,
    picking apples.
They had a camp there.
And on Sunday morning,
  about nine o'clock,
    then the people, some of 'em,
      they said,

    "It was Sunday today
      but we better go to work."

Because they, whoever they owns the apples,
  they were in a hurry, you know.
They want to get the apples taken away
  as soon's they can get them out of there.
And the other people, they said,

    "To heck with the apples.
      We're going to play stick game."

So the other people,
  they play stick game.
And the other people go out and pick apples.
They pick apples till noon.
They pick apples in the afternoon,
  about three o'clock in the afternoon.
And one lady,
  not pretty old,
    could be around sixty, I guess.
Still work, you know.
They still pick apples.
Then she put the ladder to the apples.
The ladder was only one in one side.
And they puts that through the trees.
They put them over there.
But she didn't know,

they never touch the ground.
About six inch more to hit the ground.
But it's stuck on a limb.
She did not know that.
But they climb on that ladder.
And they picks apples, here,
    the apple bag, you know.
They over the shoulders
    and then you pick apples
        and they get big here.
Heavy.
It weighs about twenty pounds or more.
And then, when it get heavy,
    then still they reach for another one
        or two.
They kind of put their weight there.

Then this leg, you know.
It was stuck there,
    but they go a little more.
And that lady,
    it just like somebody throw 'em off the ladder.
Almost to the top.
And she landed in the ground
    on her back.
Then there was a ditch about this deep, you know.
That's where she landed.
Hard, you know.
Because they's high.
Like this ceiling.
Maybe just above this ceiling.
Then they went off.
Landed on the ground.
On her back.
But they got a kind of a crack inside of 'em,
    I guess, and they spit
        and they puke the blood.

Then, right away they say,

"Go and get the Indian doctor
    to get the blood out."

So the Indian doctor,
    the one that can do that,
        she was there.
So she come.
It was another lady.
Then she suck this blood out of the other lady,
    the one that got hurt.
Suck the blood out.
And then she's all right,
    but took them back to the camp
        and put 'em to bed.

So, that was in the afternoon on Sunday,
    about three o'clock.
It happens then.
But she come home.
Come to our camp about five o'clock.
Then,

        "Well," she says.
        "I have a little news."

She says,

        "There was one lady who fell off the ladder
            and then they got hurt.
        And they were bleeding.
        But the Indian doctor was right there
            and they take the blood out.
        And she's all right."

Well, that's the one they mentioned in yesterday morning,
    before she leave.
She says it's going to be blood.
Around, not that place, but not too far from there.
Maybe today, maybe tomorrow.
But anyway, that comes on Sunday.

That was the next day.
See, every word she says,
   it's all true.
So I think she's a really good doctor.

And not only that,
   but another one, after that,
      in wintertime.
After that, after we pick apples
   and we come back
      and this woman, my woman,
         I left 'em in a mission school
            so they could sweep the floor
               and do some kind of work at the mission.

Wendy: Where was that?

That's in Omak mission.
There was a mission in Omak.
Not where we was
   but about—
      oh, five miles from there to the east,
         towards Nespelem.
In that road.

(We didn't go on that road.
Oh yes, we did.
Randy and you—
   remember when we all go together—
   when we finished the rodeo?
Then that Michael, whatever you call 'em,
   he come on my truck.
Remember?
To Penticton.
But you and Randy,
   we go to Grand Coulee and camp there.
And that is the way we go.
But that's the first time I went through that road.
But you didn't remember that.

That's over there from Omak.
That's another road, that way.)

But this time, we go to Monse.
That's in another road.
But you still will get to Grand Coulee.
See, this is the road that gets to Grand Coulee.

And we went to the mission
    and I found a job for her.
I tell the priest,
    this lady, I want 'em to be here
        so if you can give 'em a job.
All right.
The priest said,

    "All right.
        They can do the work.
        They can sweep the floors.
        Clean up the things, you know, every day.
        That'll be all right."

So I left her there.

And then, I and Awk-MEEN,
    we were there for a while.
But she went to Nespelem
    and I wait for her.
Ride my horse.
When she come back from there . . .
There was a meeting over there,
    that's why they went.
When she come back from there
    and then she could come back on the buggy
        but I take my saddle horse
            and I come home.
I come home ahead of her.
I was home about three, four days
    before she get back.
And that winter . . .

That was in the fall.
When we come back from Omak
   that was about almost end of October.
But that winter,
   and her house . . .
I was working for one ranch just about a mile
   from her house.
This way.
And I stay there.
I sleep there,
   where I work.
And I had that saddle horse.
I had that with me
   but it's turned loose in the field
      with the other horses.
Lots of horses.

And I work for this ranch.
In the winter, about—
   somewhere around about in January,
      or almost the end of January,
         and there was the moonlight.
And then my horse,
   every night that they come—
      there was a window like that,
         not as high—
            the window was lower than this—
               and I got the bed right on the floor,
               with a mattress, you know.
My head is right to the window.
Almost.
But the window is higher than my head.
And the other guy,
   they sleep in a little bed,
      narrow bed.
Just alongside of me.
And close to the wall, like that.
And my horse, they come,
   stoop right at the window
      from the outside.

Then they paw.
We could heard them, you know.
They dig the ground
and they paw.
Then I get up and I go outside
and I chase 'em away
and I gets some little stones or sticks
and chase 'em away.
Then I come back and go to bed.
Just about sleep.
Then they come back.
Then they stand there
and then paw.
Then they put their nose right at the window.
Not every night,
but every other night.
One night, never come.
Next night, they do that all night.
I chase 'em two, three times before morning.

And I was wondering,
why did they do that?
The other horses never come round.
But only them.
But that's a sign from something bad.
And I didn't know.
So, I was working,
cutting some rails.
One day, Awk-MEEN, she was coming round
on horseback
and then they come to me
where I work.
Out in the bush, you know.
I'm cutting rails.
She comes there and she says to me,

"I come to let you know.
That I'm going to put up a powwow.
I'm going to start tonight.

And it's going to be three nights.
I'm going to start it tonight.
And I want you to come.
Tonight.
Every night you're going to come to my powwow.
There's going to be some more people."

"All right," I said.
"I will go."

So, I go back to the house
   and eat supper
      and I says to these people—
         because I sleep there, you know—
I says,

"I'm going to leave.
   I'm going over there for the powwow.
   I got to go over there three nights.
   I come back in the morning."

So I went.
And I get to her place
   and there's some other people—
      not pretty many.
But anyway, she sing the song
   and we dance.
Sing the song.
And we dance.
For about after middle night.
We eat at middle night
   and then after that
      and we dance a few rounds.
A few more.
Somewhere around, about two o'clock in the morning.
Stop, and then she said to me.
She said to me,

"You come here."

And I went.
And I sat alongside of her.
She says,

> "Now, after little while,
>   another few minutes,
>   I get up and sing my song
>   and I go round that post there."

(You see that post there.
You know that post that they goes round
  and the doctor grabs that.
They have one like that.)

She says,

> "I get up and I go around this post.
>   As soon's I get up and sing my song,
>   then you can get up
>   and then you can follow me.
>   You can be behind me.
>   We can go around that post four times.
>   Then we'll stop
>   and then I can talk to you.
>   Then after that,
>   and everybody can dance."

All right.
That just special for us.
So she started to sing her song.
Then she get up and walked.
Then I get up, right away,
  and I walked behind her.
Then we go around that post.
Sing her song.
We go around, not fast, pretty slow.
You see them doctor,
  they walk there pretty slow.
S-l-o-w and then they go round.
We do the same.

Four times we go round.
Then we stop.
And sat down.
She says to me,

> "You're in a bad shape.
>> Some bad people, bad ladies,
>>> they do some witchcraft on you,
>>>> so you can be bad luck,
>>>>> or maybe you can be die that way.
>> That's what I find out.
>> But now I'm going to work on you."

What I got to say?
Because I just say, "Yes."
"Yes."
And she says,

> "Your horse,
>> they comes to where you sleep almost every night,
>>> isn't it?"

I said, "Yeah."

She says,

> "You know your horse comes there."

> "Oh," said I,
>> "yeah, because they making noise
>>> and I chase 'em.
>> Next night they never come.
>> But next night they come.
>> Going that way for two, three weeks."

She says to me,

> "Did you know why did they do that?"

I said,

"No. I don't know."

She says to me,

>"They come to let you know about what—
>   to warn you.
>   And he lets you know
>   you get in the bad way.
>   Then you going to die that way.
>   Maybe not right away
>   but they going to be in bad way
>   till you die.
>   Your horse is coming to let you know that.
>   But you go out and get a stick
>   and go after 'em.
>   That's not good.
>   You should leave it there.
>   Shouldn't chase 'em.
>   Let 'em stay."

But she says,

>"Now, they never going to come there.
>   But I'm going to do the work on you.
>   Now.
>   And next night.
>   And next night,
>   when I finished
>   and see what it'll happen."

So the next night...
She work, you know.
They work on me.
The next night I get back there.
The same thing, you know.
I always followed her four times.
But one time—
    and then the other people dance.
But on the last night,
    that's the finish,

then, towards morning,
   about two o'clock in the morning,
      three o'clock in the morning,
         she was singing.
Then, she said to me,

"Your horse is dead.
He died.
It's his idea,
   they figure that out for two days.
And he says, himself was an animal.
Better put down himself and die.
Because he's an animal.
But you're a person.
They want you to live.
For long time.
But he's a animal.
He think it may be better off for him to die.
But you can live.
But now he's dead.
He died already.
The way they want.
He died."

"So," they says,
"After a while,
   when it gets daylight,
      just begin to daylight
         and then you can go out.
You could sing my song.
Before you go out.
Then you can keep sing that song
   then you go that way."

There was a field,
  a lot of bushes, you know,
    a big place and a big bush in the middle
    and there was a road—
      this way.
And there's another road this way.

But she don't tell me where the horse dead.
She says,

"They die."

She says,

"You sing my song and you go.
    And you going to run into that horse.
    It's laying already,
        they die.
    But you going to run into 'em.
    When you see 'em,
        when you run into 'em,
            you stop and take a good look.
    If their head like to the west,
        they kind of lay that way,
            his head to the west,
                and that's bad.
    And just see his head to the west
        and then you just get going.
    We should say that means good-bye.
    But if you see his head to the east,
        then you stop right on his head,
            and you facing to the west,
                but your horse is facing to the east,
                you stand right on his head.
    And you talk to 'em."

And then she tell me what to say.

She says,

"You say this.
    You talk to your horse.
    You talk to 'em there for a little while
        and then you tell 'em,
            'You going to be there for three days.
    And then I'll come and get you
        and I'll put you in the place

where you're going to be for all time.'
That's what you're going to tell 'em
and then you tell 'em
to help you as much as they can do for you
so you can live—
for long time.
Because he's dropped himself.
He want to be that way.
But he wants you to live.
But still you got to tell 'em.
Then, when you leave,
and don't look back,
you go to where you're going
and never look back
till you go out of the side.

"Three days, it's about ten o'clock in the morning.
The sun will be way up.
You bring the team of horses
and the wagon.
Then you tie 'em with a chain here.
And tie 'em to the wagon
and drag 'em to the place
where it's kind of low.
Low, low place,
kind of gully or something.
Then you leave 'em there.
When he get rotten,
when he get all their bone,
when they go to part—
they can be still together in the whole, like.
But if you throw 'em someplace,
then maybe coyote, maybe dog—
they might drag the bone
and scatter them all over
but this way they can stay in one hole
for long, long time before they be no more."

All right.
I went.

I sing the song.
In the house, I sing.
Then I go out
    and I keep singing the song.
And I went about a mile,
    I walked.
Then I stop and I thought,
    now, where do I have to go?
She didn't tell me:
    this is the road, this way.
And this is another road, this way.
Supposing if I go this way,
    he might've be over here.
If I go that way,
    they might've be over here.
And how can I find 'em?

I don't know what to do.
I stood there a while and figure out.
Well, I thought,
    I turn to my right and go that way
        for a chance.
So I went that way.
I walked another three hundred yards.
And a little bunch of bush in a strip.
And they got kind of a point over there.
And I come here.
And then I have to go around that little bunch of bushes.
As soon's I go around,
    then I see the horse.
Were laying just a little ways.
When I go around there,
    it was daylight already.
And I seen the horse was laying.
Facing to the east.
The way she tell me.
Or else, could be facing to the west.
And that's bad.

So anyway, I stop
   and stood right on the front of his head, you know.
I facing to the west,
   but he's facing that way.
And I stand on his head right here.
And I talk to 'em.
I says,

    "Yeah, you finished off yourself
       because you want it that way.
     That was your own idea.
     Now you're dead.
     I bet you stay there for three days.
     But in the morning when the sun was up,
       I'm going to come on a team of horses
         and I'm going to move you from here.
     I know where I'm going to put you—
       in the gully so you can be there
         for the rest of time."

That's what I say,
   but in Indian, you know.
Not in English.
So I left.
And I go to where I'm going—
   to the house where I work.
I never look back.
I keep going till I get out of the sight
   and then I keep going till I get back to house
     and I eat.
I never said nothing.
Three days.
On the third day,
   then we went and feed the cattle,
     and I tell my boss,

    "I want the team.
      When we get through,

I'm going to take the team.
My horse is dead
and I'm going to drag them where they was."

He said,

"All right. You can do that."

So when we're finished the feeding,
and I drive the team
and I get to that horse
and I take the chain along.
And I put the chain on his neck
and I hook 'em to the wagon
and I drag 'em a little ways,
about two, three hundred yards.
And it was kind of a gully
and I left 'em there.
I stop and I talk to 'em
and I says,

"You going to be here the rest of the time.
When your bone—
when your body rotten—
when your bones are spread all over,
you know, they comes apart,
but still they'd be in the gully.
You can be in the gully there for all time."

So I left.
And there's another thing.
When we had the powwow,
on the second night—
no, on the first night—
and I come back.
And after breakfast we go out
and feed the cows.
And we load up hay.
But we see the cattle is on the railroad track.
The some.

But some is where we was.
But some of 'em is in the railroad track.
And before I left,
   and she says to me,

     "I want you to kill a bird.
       Some kind of bird,
         maybe a willow grouse,
         or maybe the quail."

There used to be . . . the quail.
Smaller than the grouse.
They call 'em the quail.
He says,

     "Either you can get the quail or pheasant,
       or willow grouse,
         either one of 'em,
           I want you to kill 'em.
     When you kill them.
     Right away,
       as soon's you kill them,
         you bring them.
     And I want to eat them.
     Before night."

     "All right," I says,
     "I do that.
       And I come."

Then we go out and feed the cows.
And I forgot.
But the cattle is in the railroad track.
Some.
About twenty head.
And my boss says to me,

     "The train is coming.
       They whistle.
       You better go over there

and you go over the railroad track.
Don't let them see you
    but you can go over the track
        because the railroad is built high."

He says,

    "You can run on the other side on the field.
      Till you think you past,
         then you can get on the track
           and then you can scare them
             and then they will run.
    And leave the gate open.
    Scare them and then they will run.
    When they come to the gate,
      it'll all come out.
    The train is coming."

I said, "All right."

And then I went.
And I go over the track
  and I leave the gate open in one side
    and I close the other side.
I went to where they going to go out
  and I leave that open.
Then I run on the other side
  and then I think I passed 'em already.
And I get on the track.
And I did pass them.
So I scared them.
I take some stone and throw them.
And they run.
They all run.
Along the fence.
Because the railroad, they got the fence on each side.

Pretty soon they scare the little quails.
And they fly over the track.
It just from there—

and just over the rock.
And then they landed again on this side.
A bunch of 'em.
And then I begin to know
   that I supposed to kill a bird that day.
And here's my chance.
There's bird there.
I got no gun,
   I got nothing,
      but anyway I pick up a stone.
About this size.
And I seen 'em just where they landed.
And I just throw the stone that way.
And one of 'em,
   I hit 'em right in the back.
I didn't see 'em.
I just throw the stone that way.
But I hit the one of 'em right in the back.

And, that time, I run down.
And this bird,
   I could see them still moving.
Then I get there
   and I just about picking 'em up
      then he's dead.
That little, they were small.
They call 'em the quail.

Then, I thought I supposed to take this bird
   right away to her.
So I get back
   and the train is getting closer
      and the cows they run
         and they run out.
And my boss, they throw some hay on.
Before I get there.
Then, when I come to him,
   then he just give me the line
      and I'm walking

and he threw the hay off.
So we finished feeding
  and I says to him,

    "This is what I supposed to do
      and I got the bird.
    I have the bird here.
    I supposed to take this bird to her right now.
    You take the team back
      and I go over there
        and I'll come back in an hour or so.
    Then I can go to work again."

He said,

    "All right."

He says,

    "You go ahead."

So I go right from there.
Then he brings the team back.
Then I run—
  just about a mile.
And I get there
  and she was in the house,
    and she were cooking.

    "Well," I says,
    "here's the bird.
      I get 'em."

    "By gosh," she says,
    "that was good.
      That was all right.
      I thought maybe you forget,
        maybe you never get 'em."

I says,

"I did forget but I seen the birds a-flying.
   Then I come to know I supposed to get one of 'em
      and I just taking a chance
         and I did get one."

She laugh and she says,

   "That was a good luck."

So that's one of 'em,
   she was saying,
      for me to do,
         and it comes true.
I did kill one.
And she eat 'em.
That's her power.

She want to be that way.
See, whatever she says, they always true.
They never tell a lie.
They tell something
   and it comes true—right.
She knows.

And then, when we're finished,
   that was the time before I see the horse was dead,
      while I'm still in the house.
But she says to me,

   "You could sing my song.
      In the house.
      And then you go out.
      And then keep singing till you find the horse."

That's what she tell me.
And then she says,

   "Now.
      We okay.
      We out of it.

Everything.
But, you never know.
You might get hurt one of these days.
Maybe not.
Maybe long time from now.
But whenever you get hurt sometimes,
  maybe long time from now
    and don't forget my song.
When you get hurt
  you know you get hurt,
    then you could sing my song.
And that'll help you.
Even if I'm a-living or not.
But still you can sing my song
  whenever you get hurt."

She says,

"You never know.
  You might get hurt sometimes."

PART IV

ENCOUNTERS
WITH POWER

YOU CAN'T SEE ME, BUT JUST LISTEN

While hunting, a man hears a voice that warns him of strange things to come.

That story, it become just about 1920.
Or maybe a little before.
When it comes, that story.
That's down in Oregon somewhere.
In those days, there was a road.
But no paved,
   we never see that.
We don't know.
All roads at everywhere,
   no paved road.
But just a gravel road,
   and kind of rough.
Kind of narrow.
We never see that till quite a ways,
   about 1945 or '46,
   when we see the paved road.
But about the 1920,
   and down in Oregon somewhere.
And there was a bunch of Indians,
   either they had a tepee,
     or they got some houses,
   in one part, like.
More like—something like Penticton, you know.

They all together, like.
Just a bunch of houses.
In one spot.

And, on the mountain,
    not very high.
And, once in a while, the mans,
    they go up that way
        and do the hunting.
They got some deer.
They always hunt deer
    and antelope.
And this time, and one of the boys,
    one of the mans,
        they wanted to hunt,
            and he asked some of the other ones,
                said,

    "Maybe we better go hunting."

They wanted to go,
    about two, three man.
Go up and hunt.
But no,
    nobody went with 'em.
So they thought,
    well, they thought they can hunt
        just by himself alone.
They couldn't get nobody to go with 'em.
But he think,
    he can go alone.
So he went.
One morning.
He went up the hill—
    it's not pretty steep,
        not like this.
It's just kind of.
And he get up to the top,
    and another kind of valley that way,

like from the right.
And the valley seems to go around.
Turn that way.
And this is kind of a mountain.
When he get on top,
  so he could see,
    long ways.
Then he stop.
Then he look,
  like that way—
      he look ahead.
And he decided the trails,
  he thought they can go,
    go way over there
      and then he would turn
        and make a circle.
Go that way.
Keep going that way
  and go home.
He might see some deer.
He look at the place where he should go.
No timber, no trees.
But there was some bushes,
  willow bush.
Poplar, sagebrush, in places.
There was—
  in places it was damp, you know.
And they got some spring water in places.
There should be deer.
So he look at the place,
  and then,

    "I'm going that way."

He decided where he should go.

So he started.
He just move.
Move, so they'll go.

As soon's he move,
  he could hear the voice.
Somebody told 'em,

>   "Wait a minute.
>   I'm going to tell you something.
>   Stop and turn around.
>   Look."

Sounds like from behind.
Looked around and he don't see no one.
Nothing.
Then, still they told 'em,
  said,

>   "You can't see me.
>   You can't see me
>   but just listen to me.
>   I'll tell you something."

Sounds like.
And high.
So he stop and wait.
And whoever they are talking to 'em,
  they tell 'em,

>   "You think you wanted to go from there
>   over there
>   and make a turn
>   and go that way.
>   That's what you think you should go?"

And he said,

>   "Yeah.
>   "I think I should go that way."

And, they told 'em,

"You're not to go that way—
    the way you think you should go.

"You can turn to your right.
   Then you can go over there
    and you could see that big rock.
   About half a mile from here."

There was a big rock.
Big boulder.
But it's kind of flat on top.
It's not flat,
  it's not level.
Kind of sloping.
It's kind of flat, you know.
The rock was high.
A big one.
They could see that for long ways.
About half a mile or more.
Told 'em,

"You can go to that rock.
   Instead of go to where you think you should go,
    go to this rock.
   You can go to get to that rock.
   Then you look on that rock.
   You might see something right on the rock.
   If you do, go on,
    pick 'em up and take a look.
   But put 'em back the same way.
   And then you can look to your right.
   Stay to your right.
   Then you might see something.
   Couldn't be too far from that rock."

That's what they told 'em.
All right.
That's all.

He turn around
  and he went to that rock.
He walking and walking and walking.
He come to the rock.
He looked around,
  he don't see nothing.
But only the rock.
And he look on the rock.
Then he see shoes.
Man's shoes.
Only one.
That's supposed to be working shoe.
But it's high top.
To here.
And it lay on that rock.
And it must've been lay that rock quite a while.
And it get kind of change colour from the sun.
To the other side.
But the other side,
  it was the same colour, like.
They must've been lay there quite a while.
So he picked that up
  and looked at 'em.
He thinks these shoes must've been lay there long time.
The top side was changed colour.
But he put 'em back the same.
And he think,
  he think,

    "I was told to put this back.
      I supposed to look to the right.
      I might see something. "

So he turned around and look to the right,
  not too far.
And then he see the road.
There was a road.
Like, up towards uphill.
Straight to the east.

And the road to the west—
   this is kind of a gully, you know—
      kind of a valley.
That's where he was,
   in the bottom of the valley.
Then they see the road
   and from there the road was kind of uphill.
From the other one,
   kind of uphill too.
And he seen the road.
They different.
The road.

And he could see,
   from where he was standing,
      straight to where he was.
The road, that's the end,
   right there.
And this one is the end.
But this one here,
   it just open, right, straight through.
No road.
As far as the road goes.
Quite, quite a ways.
Far.
Maybe wider than this house.
So he thinks that he can walk over there,
   and then he can come to 'em.
He might feel it, you know.
He wants to know what it was.
So he went over there.
He couldn't get near it.
Just about like from here to that wall.
He walked and walked
   and walked
      and walked.
Still he couldn't get closer.
Then he stop and look.
Then he see that rock,

they passed quite a ways up the hill.
Then he could see the road.
Coming past that rock.
And it was right behind,
   just about the same.
So he thought,

     "Well, I'll go back and follow this one.
      I might caught up to 'em."

So he go back
   and he going to catch that,
     and keep going
       and still he never get near it.
The first thing they know,
   he go past that big rock again,
     the other way.
And look.
A road was coming by.
That rock.
That's supposed to be open right out.
So, he come back.
Come back and he come by again.
By the rock, you know,
   right here.
And he come there,
   and, then, same way.
Road that way.
And road that way.
And it's open, right out.
Then he walk to the rock and stand there.
And he look—
   still the same.

Then, he heard the voice again.
Told 'em,

     "Now you see that road.
      You see that road,

    that road, it's right from the west coast
       and right over to the east coast.
And, is going to be another one.
From north, and right to the south.
And, it's going to go across like that.
And that's going to be the road.
When that would happen,
    the other one goes across to this road,
       and after that they going to build a road everywhere,
         every place, even on the mountain,
           on the high mountain.
They can build the road everywhere.
They just like that.
It's going to be that blacktop you see.
Wide.
They can be that way.
Not now, not right away,
    but later on.
Maybe a few years from now.
You might see that.
You may not.
You might be dead before that come.
    But that's the way it's going to be.
    This road from the west to the east coast
       and from the north to the south.
They went across like that.
But after that,
    will be road everywhere."

All right.
That's all.
So, they told 'em,

    "When you get back home,
       you'll tell your people what you have seen here.
    If they don't believe you,
       if they want to see,
         they can come, with you.
    They might see that shoes.

But they may not see the road by that time.
Or maybe they see it.
Nobody know."

So, that's the last.
And he come.
He go back the same way.
And then he go to where they figure he should go to hunt.
And he went that way.
Get home.
He never see no deer or nothing.
And he get home.
And then he tell some of the friend,
   and he tell 'em,

     "You better tell the others,
        let 'em come here.
       Then I'm going to tell 'em what I see.
       And what I heard."

So they tell the other people.
Pretty soon, they—bunch of 'em—come.
They gathered, you know.
Then, he was telling 'em what he had seen.
They heard somebody talking to 'em
   and tell 'em where to go.
Then he see that shoes.
And then he see the road.
And he see that they couldn't caught up to the road.
In both ways.
So, some of 'em, they told 'em,

     "It's the only way is to go with you tomorrow.
       Then we can see that rock.
       See if the shoes is there.
       And see if we could see that road."

And they told 'em,
   he was told,

"May see the road,
    may not."

So anyway, tomorrow they went.
About three or four of 'em.
Or maybe more.

They go and they come to the place.
Then they said,

    "I stop here.
      And I was just going to go
        and somebody talk to me.
      And they tell me to go to that rock."

And then they could see the rock from there.
So they went.
When they come to the rock,
    and that shoes is still there.
Still on the rock.
But they never see no road
    the other side of the rock, or nothing.
But the shoes is still there.
And one of the man, they were with 'em,
    take the shoes and look at 'em.
And he says,

    "Maybe some prospector going by through here,
        maybe they leading a pack horse,
            and these shoes,
                it might've be tied on top of the pack.
        Somehow that they unloosed and drop one off.
        Down here near the rock.
        But whoever, they don't know,
            they keep going.
        Maybe in a few days,
            maybe another prospector going by,
                found that shoes,
                    lay there somewhere.

They might've think,
  whoever lose this shoe,
    they might track back,
      so I'm going to take 'em
        and put 'em on the rock.
Because they will look at the rock anyway.
They can find the shoes.
So they picks 'em up
  and put 'em on that rock.
And nobody come to look for that shoes.
That shoes is been there a long time.
That's the way it happens with that shoe.
But where is the road?"

So they went, and he says,

  "Right here.
  From here and the road straight over the mountain.
  This way, straight over the mountain.
  But now, it's not there."

And he said, he was told,
  that's the way it's going to be.
Later on, it's going to be road something like that.
That the way it's going to be,
  look like.
That was about the 1920.
Or maybe before that.
Then, a few years after that,
  we see that.
Now it's all over.
Now you see they going to build the road
  in the new place, like.
There's lots of 'em like that,
  everywhere.
Just like the way he says.
But he might've been dead.
He never see that.
But we do.
We heard that.

I heard that a long time.
Then, when I first heard that,
    I thought, well maybe—
        may not.
But now, I think,
    by God they was right.
We can see the road like that everywhere.
So whoever they see that,
    somebody told 'em,
        they was right.
He's not dreaming.
That's not his dream.
They just somebody told 'em.
But then only is, they never see
    whoever tell them.
That's one way can be that.

THE INDIANS, THEY
GOT THE POWER

When the trains first went through Sicamous, the Shuswap people living close by found the noise very disturbing. So they devised a way to receive compensation for the disturbance.

White boy, he
   raised with the Indians.
He was amongst the Indians.
He lived there till he get big.
Till he get to be man.
And then some of the white man,
   they took him, you know.
They took him away from the Indians.
And they took 'em on their side
   and teach 'em so they can go to school, you know.
But, he knows all about the Indian way.
Because he grew up among those Indians.

And when the train come along,
   built the railroad from over there,
      and they come through Kamloops.
Then they come through the Sicamous.
The train come through Sicamous
   and they kept a-comin'
      and they went as far as Lytton somewhere,
         you know, that way.
But they still makin' the railroad ahead of them, you know.
But the train, it comes that way so far.

Now, in Sicamous, somewhere there,
  there was a lot of Indians.
That's Shuswap, you know—Sicamous is Shuswap.
Now, the train comes along.
The freight train, and the passenger.
They makin' lot of noise, you know,
  when the train go by and they blow the horn.
And they make a lot of noise goin' by.
And these Indians, they don't like that.

And this white man,
  the one that's raised in the Indian way in the prairie,
    he's workin' in the train crew.
Like the freight train.
I think it was the freight train.
He's workin' there.
But he knows all the Indian way.

Then one day, there's about four, five,
  maybe six, Indian, all Indian doctors.
Power mans.
They get together,
  and then they have a meetin'
    and then they says,

    "We're goin' to stop the train.
      They give us so much noise.
      We don't like it to go by.
      We're goin' to stop it."

And the other one said,

    "How are you goin' to stop 'em?"

    "Well, put somethin' on the railroad track.
      And when they get there,
        then they wouldn't go no more."

Then the other one ask them,

"What're you goin' to put there?"

"Well," he says, "a grizzly bear.
    I put the grizzly bear there."

"No," the other one says.
"That grizzly bear,
        the train'll hit 'em
            and they'll cut 'em in pieces and kill 'em.
    You can't use that."

"Ah," the other one says.
"I think I can do it."

"Well, what you goin' to put there?"

He says,
        "I'll put that moose.
            The moose, you know, they big animal."

He says,

        "I'll put the moose there
            and then when the train hits that moose
            and then the moose—"

"Oh, no. That moose is like a nothin'.
    That train goin' ride over 'em
        and tore 'em into pieces."

They ask one another what they goin' to put there
    to stop the train.
And the other one, the last one,
    they asked him.

"What're you goin' to do?"

"Well," he says, "I put the groundhog there.
    On the track.
    And then the train wouldn't go."

"Oh, go on.
   The grizzly is big,
      but still the train'll smash 'em when he hit 'em.
   And the moose is big,
      but the train'll hit 'em and smash.
   But the groundhog—
      how he goin' to stop the train?"

Well, all right.

"Not only the groundhog, but the big, big boulder.
   The big boulder with 'em because the big boulder—
      the great big boulder—
         the groundhog, they always lay on that boulder.
   And I'm goin' to set that boulder right on the track.
   And the groundhog can be on that boulder.
   And the train wouldn't move that boulder."

They say,

"All right. Go to it.
   We'll see if you can make it."

So they put it.
That's his power.
The Indian, they call that shoo-MISH.
So they put that,
   and then they went away from the track a little ways.
And they stop.
And they sat down and make a fire
   and then they play stick game.
They want to see what the train is going to do
   when they go by.
They know they comin'.
In the afternoon.
The train goes through there 'bout four o'clock in the
   afternoon.
Then they waitin' for the train.
And they already put that big boulder on the track.
So they play stick game not too far from the railroad.

Now, here's the freight train.
They comes along and then they must've hit that boulder.
They was a-runnin'.
Then they stop.
And they stop
   and the wheel was spinnin'.

They back the train, you know.
They put 'em in reverse.
And back for quite a ways.
And then they go from there.
They thought they goin' to go right through.
And they go fast.
Same place, and then they stop.
And then they just stop
   and they try to make 'em go
      and the wheels was a-spinning.
They couldn't go.
My God!
They backed 'em again.
Quite a ways.
Then go again.
They thought they going to go fast.
They never seen nothin' on that track.
But they could see where the rails—
   where the wheel was spinning.
But they don't see nothin'.
Till two, three times
   and they couldn't go.

They comes to same place and stop.
The wheel was spinning.
And this man, that white man that one that grow up
   with the Indians, he's in the bunch.
He's workin' on that crew.
Then they said to the other workers,
   they said,

    "I know why."

He says,

> "These Indians over there,
>> bunch over there, they was sitting there.
> He's the one that makes that.
> They must've put something on that track.
> Maybe you guys should get a lot of this food.
> Maybe bacon, rice and stuff like that, smoke, tobacco."

It used to be that the tobacco in rolls,
> like a rope,
>> and they, lot of them.
They must've been freight train,
> because they was hauling a lot of stuff, you know.

> "Get some of that stuff
>> and put 'em in the box
>>> and pack them over there.
> And get to this mans and tell 'em,
>> 'This one here, we give you.
>> We pay you.
>> Let us go by.
>> You take this stuff.
>> It's yours.
>> We give it to you.
>> But let us go by.'
> They'll take it.
> And they let you go by."

They couldn't believe it, you know.
They couldn't believe him.
So they tell him again.

They says,

> "I know all about the Indian way.
>> These is the guys.
>> That's why they was settin' there.
>> They was waiting there to see

> if the train stuck or keep going.
> Now that they know, they stops 'em,
>> if you don't pay them for you to go by
>> and what you going to do?
> Your train is quit right here.
> By these mans."

All right.
This other one, they,

> "All right. We'll try that one."

So they get all the food.
Bacon, potatoes and rice
  and some other stuff.
Every one of 'em, they had a big pack.
And they go over there.
And they get to that Indians and tell 'em,

> "We give you this food and tobacco
>> and everything.
> Matches.
> And let us go by.
> You can take these.
> We pay you for this.
> Will let us go by?"

> "All right. Okay.
> We'll let you go by."

So they all walked over there.
Then these white people, they stop and watch 'em.
And these Indians they walked over there
  and they sing their song
    and walk around
      and then they go over across the track
        and walk around.
After a while, they walked over there a little ways
  and stopped.

"All right. Okay.
    You guys go."

So they start the train, you know.
They backed 'em little bit, then go.
They kept goin'.
So they, they put that boulder.
That's why that train hit that boulder,
    they couldn't move 'em.
And they couldn't—
    that's why the wheel was spinning.
That's a hard to believe,
    but the Indians they can do.
Yeah. They got the power.
They can do that.

BIG MAN PUTS
THE POWER ON
A HEDLEY BOY

Two hunters and a young boy go hunting. After killing a deer, the men
ask the boy to carry the meat home. En route, the boy is distracted by
what he thinks is a squirrel.

The Indians, they had a camp.
Over there, where that church is now.
And down that way, towards the river.
That's where they had a camp.
A lot of Indians.
And they have a camp there,
   and they go up hunting.
Up to where they call the—Nickle Bridge Road—
   is now, they call it.
But there was a trail there, those days.
So the Indians they go out hunting that way.
And supposing if we over there by the church.
I could tell you just whereabouts.
And the boys, could be about fourteen years old—
   maybe not,
      maybe only twelve—something like that.
And they take that boy along with them.
The two men, and that boy.
And they went up hunting,
   up to the top, and they kill deer.
And this deer was just a fawn.

Not very big.
A yearling, or something.
They kill this fawn
  and then they skin 'em
    and cut 'em in pieces
      and then they put them in the skin.
And they know how to fix 'em so that boy can pack 'em.
And he pack 'em on his back.
Then they come down.
They tell 'em,

    "You packs this meat and then you go down.
      Go home. Go to the camp."

But he says, the older fellow,

    "We go round the gully over here.
      We going to hunt on the way that way,
        and then we get down.
      But you just pack this one and go home."

So this boy, he started to pack that meat,
  and he come down about halfways.
That's not too far.
If he could see, right from the church.
That little ridge up on the hillside.
And they used to tell me just whereabouts.
And they were coming down there.
And then they heard this squirrel.
This squirrel was singing, you know.
This squirrel—he on the tree, you know.
You could hear—

You heard the squirrel?

    Wendy: Yeah.

And then he heard that.
And then he stopped.
And they listen.

And then it sounds—not like squirrel.
Sounds a little different.
But in other way, sounds like a squirrel.
But still, it's not, not like a squirrel.
It's a little different.
So he thought to himself,
  he was wondering what that is.
So he take off his pack
  and lay it on the ground right on the trail.
And he heard this squirrel not too far
  in the timber.
So he went over there.
He like to see 'em.
He thought he might find 'em.

He walked that way and looked around.
First thing he knew,
  he see a man standing there.
Big, big man.
Tall.
There was a hair all over, you know.
The neck was big, but he was short.
And so he see 'em,
  he just went to sleep.
And this gorilla,
  they put the power on 'em.
And he just fall.
And they sticking up
  and the gorilla, they pick 'em up
    and put 'em on the gorilla's shoulders.
And packed 'em.
And down they went,
  and then the other side of the church,
    just before you go up to that little hill there by the
      cemetery.
And that's where the gorilla went across,
  when they track 'em.

And this time, this other mens come back
  and get to the camp.

"And where's the boy?"

He says,

"He never come."

He says,

"We sent 'em.
    We sent him home.
    But we went way 'round and we come back.
    He should've been here."

"No. He never come."

They miss that boy all night.
Getting dark, you know.
He never show up.
He never get back to the camp.
Next morning they went up to see if...
They thought he might get hurt or something.
They went up on the trail.
Finally they found his pack.
He take the pack up and he lay them there.
And they looked for tracks
    and they could see his tracks.
Towards the timber.
And they went over there
    and they could see the other tracks,
        about this big.
That's the gorilla track, you know, barefooted.

Then they followed that.
Followed that until they come to the river.
Then they crossed the river.
Then they followed 'em and they go up the hill.
And way up to the top
    and then they lost the track.
Because in the mountain,
    in the timber,

and then they couldn't see the track no more.
They missed that boy altogether.
They don't know what happens.
They know the gorilla take him.
They thought he might've kill 'em.

Long time after that,
    and they sent the word from Yakima.
They were gathering to play stick game.
The people gathered, you know, the Indians.
And some of the Indians from here go that way.
And they send a word.
They say,

    "We got a stranger here.
        Supposed to be coming from up there."

And this gorilla then pack that boy—
    if I had a map I could show you on the map.
There was a map in there.
I could show you just where they left 'em.
Yeah.
They packs that boy from Hedley.
And then they packed him that far.
Then right along the lake
    and he left 'em there.
And there was an Indian at a camp on the end of the lake.
I don't know which way,
    but it's likely in the end of the lake.
And they had a camp.
A lot of Indians.
And these Indians, they had a camp
    and they make fire
        and they got the smoke.
You know, the fire was smoking from the camp.
And they left the boy there.
Was still sleeping—
    still, you know, just like sleeping—
        and he gets kind of stiff.
So they could pack 'em.

And they left 'em there.
And this boy, he was laying there.
And he wake up.
Wake up and looked around.
He never see this place before.
He was in a strange place.
Now, he was wondering
    and he get up and looked around
        and he could see not too far there was smoke.
He think there must've been people over there.
Must be somebody live there.
That's why they got the smoke.
So he walked that way.

That's what he was saying.
When he get a bunch of Indian
    he tell all what's happened, you know.
With him.
The last he know.
They say that marked rock, they call 'em now.
That Hedley.
Used to be marked plain.
You could see 'em good,
    but now you could still see 'em
        but not so clear.
They mentioned that place
    the marked rock,
        nice looking—mark in strips.
That's the place.
Last I know, it's there.

But he wake up there
    and he could see that smoke
        and then he walked towards the smoke
            and he come round a little the lake
                and he come near the camp
                    and he could see the people,
                        could be about two, three hundred yards.
Then he stopped there.
Then these other people seen him

and they know it was a stranger.
So, they walked over there.
But when he get there,
   he sleeped again.
He don't know.
Then he went and get the medicine
   and make a fire
      and they smoked 'em.

They call that medicine HUSH-hush.
They dig 'em from the ground, little roots.
You could smell it,
   you could smell that long ways.
And they used that to get faint, like, you know.
He just went to sleep.
And he smoked 'em.
And pretty soon
   and the Indian doctors sing their song
      and they worked on 'em.
Pretty soon they come to again.
And they talked to 'em.
But they got a different language over there.
That Yakima language—than the Okanagan.

But, he stay there.
A lot of people.
And, pretty soon he get to understand on their language.
They get to understanding.
Then when they get to understanding in the Yakima language,
   then they tell all about what happened where they was.
Mention all these places.
Says,

   "That's the last that I know."

So, they knew that quite a ways.

Then, one time, when he get to be a big man,
   then he get the wife right from that bunch.
Then he get the family

and then he stay there all the time.
Then they send the word to these people
and tell 'em that,

    "There's a man here,
        he was just a boy when we found him.
    And he was still here.
    The way he was saying,
        he's from over there.
    Maybe you guys should come and see."

So finally the people from here,
    they went to Yakima on horseback.
And they met them,
    they seen 'em.
And they tell 'em,

    "We come to get you.
        To get you back, to our home country."

    "No," he says.
    "I get used to it,
        livin' here with these people.
    And I better stay here.
    I'm not going back."

They went to get 'em twice,
    but he couldn't come.
So, he stay there
    and then he died.
But he's right from here,
    but the gorilla took him all the way.
And that's a long ways.
Never comes back.
He don't want to come back
    because he had the family
        and he get used to it to be there.

SHE WAS DEAD
AT ONE TIME, BUT
SHE COME ALIVE

Some people die and come to life again.

The Indians, that's when they were imbellable★
    stories.
The way I say a while ago.
They go underground as well as the white people.
See, the white people, they go underground.
They make a tunnel.
They make a road.
Go through underground.
And they make a tunnel for the train
    to go underground.
Go underground.
Go under the mountain.
And the Indians, they go underground too.
And that's Badger and another one.
I forget the other one's name.
But Badger anyway.

Badger was the digger.
He can dig the ground and let it out, you know,

★ This is the English translation Harry was given for *chap*-TEEK-*whl*, stories from "way back" during the time of the first ancestors. Someone told Harry that the word for *chap*-TEEK-whl is "unbelievable," which he heard as "imbellable."

the digging.
Then they go in the ground.
And the other one go behind 'em
   and then they kick this all out.
And the dead body, they wanted one of them.
They wanted to marry this girl.
But whoever the daughter, whoever the folks for that girl,
   they don't want 'em.
See, they no good.
One of 'em was a Badger and the other one was a—
I know the animal, but I couldn't think of their name.
They don't want 'em.
So this animal, they knew that.
So they thought they can use their power
   to get that girl to die.
When she die, they will bury 'em.
And after she was buried, and they can dig
   and reach to her,
      when she was in the ground.
And they could bring 'em out of that tunnel
   that they make and bring 'em right out.
So they wouldn't show where they was buried.
Because from a long ways,
   and then they dig and go under the ground,
      till they reach to this woman,
         the one that's buried.
And they drag 'em and then they take 'em
   through that tunnel and take 'em out,
      way in different place.
When the people comes round the grave would the same,
   they never think it was taken out,
      but it was taken out.

And they take 'em home.
And when they get them home and they leave 'em,
   close to the water.
Part of it, it's laying in the water for overnight.
And they dance there.
And they sing their song.
The next night they went the same way.

And they get this woman to come alive.
And this woman come alive.
And they had that for wife,
     one of 'em.
So that's why, the Indians, they go underground
     as well as the white people.
See, it's beginning from that time.

And that is why, there's some Indian die
     and they come alive again.
But not pretty often.
Just a few, it happens that way.
There was one woman, she been sick for quite a while.
That's not too long ago.
That's not imbellible stories,
     that's just way back,
          while the animal people was drawn off from the animal.
After that.
While they come to be alive,
     come to alive.
And this woman was sick for quite a while
     and she get kind of poor and die.
In the camp.
And those days, whenever somebody died,
     in one camp maybe five, six tepees there.
Bunch of people, five or six tepee.
Something like that.
And one of them died,
     in that place.
And after they bury 'em, and all these people
     that's in the camp,
          they moved to another place to put in the camp.
And they leave that alone.
Nobody there.
That's what they do, those days.

When this woman died, and bury her.
No, no, no.
Not bury 'em yet.
They take 'em away.

They roll 'em in—they make this thing out of tules
    and what do you call—
I guess I forgot the name.
But anyway, they get that from a slough.
The grass about that big, but it's kind of soft.
And tall.
They put them together and then they put little rope
    and then they make a kind of a canvas.
A big one.
And they strong.
And they roll 'em in there.
Put them in there and then they roll 'em.
They good and strong.
And then they tie 'em with a strong rope,
    in by the head up here.
And they tie 'em there
    and then they might tie 'em right across here
        and then they tie 'em by the knees.
Three, three time.
And then they tie 'em on the foot.
Then they tie some other rope there
    so somebody could pack 'em, you know.

And they take them away from camp,
    about a quarter of a mile or more.
And then they would break a limb,
    green, green tree.
Green limb.
Big limb.
They cut them with a knife.
Stone knife.
They cut them and they was already cut.
Make kind of a knot right around.
And then they break it.
And then there's a butt there,
    sticking out about that long from the tree.
The limb, sticking out yet.
But the rest of 'em was cut off, broke off.
And they hang 'em there.
And they never could,

how can they come off?
They can never come off.
Unless somebody pull 'em off.
And they leave 'em there for three night.
On the third night, at that day,
    the next morning, at that morning,
        and they could take 'em somewhere in the slide,
        and they bury 'em in the slide.
They open the slide.
They take the stone away and make kind of a hole on the
    slide.
And they put the body in
    and then they put the stone on
        and then they get them all levelled
            and it don't look like anybody there.
But that's the grave.

That's what they do those days.
And this time, when this woman died,
    and they do the same.
After she died, they roll 'em in there.
And they take 'em away and hang 'em on the tree.
And her father was not too old.
Can be around seventy, seventy-five.
Strong yet.
In the morning, early in the morning,
    and then they goes over there to his daughter
        and stand there and look.
His daughter hangs on the tree.
He looked for 'em a little ways,
    looked at 'em.
Then go back.
He cry and go back.

The next morning, he go the same way.
On the third morning, he go back the same.
That was the day can be buried.
Just getting daylight, not quite good,
    kind of dark yet.
When he come to the place, and he know where,

but he never take a good look
    but he kept walking that way.
Till they gets close.
Like from here to that window.
And then he take a good look
    and his daughter is not hanging.
He don't see 'em there.
He see 'em on the ground.
Stop.
Kind of scared.
And she was sitting.
Right on the ground.
Were alive.
And the old man kind of scared and stop.
And his daughter know that he was there.

And told her dad,

    "Don't you get scared.
      Come here.
      I want to talk to you.
      That was me.
      I was sleepin' here.
      I get cold."

So the older one walked a little ways
    and come closer.
And he could see her sitting.
And all this stuff, it was rolled,
    it's laying behind 'em, like.
They sitting there and this one it's laying there,
    it's all open.
And he said to his daughter,

    "Who unhook you from there?
      And who undone this?
      It's been tied."

She says,

"I don't know.
  First thing I know, I was sittin' here.
  Then I could feel something behind me.
  I don't know what that is.
  Anyways, I'm getting cold.
  You better go back to camp fast.
  You run.
  You go fast.
  And get the other people
    and they can come, bring stretcher.
  Then they could carry me back to camp on a stretcher,
    where is warm.
  I'm getting cold."

She come alive.
He run back and told the people,
  but they couldn't believe 'em.

  "Well," he said.
  "You better come and bring the stretcher
      because I'm not going to tell lie for things like that.
    She's alive.
    Bring 'em home."

So they went over there and get there.
She was alive.
Put her in the stretcher, carry 'em back to camp,
  and she were laying around
    and still alive
      and she wanted to eat something
        and they feed 'em.
For quite a while, and then they getting stronger.
Getting stronger.
Quite a while.
And then she get better.
She can get up and walk around.
Pretty soon she was getting better just like the others.
She go with the other woman to pick berries
  and go for digging

　　and just like it was before.
She get better.

But she was dead at one time.
But they come alive.
So that is why.
Because the Badger and the other one—
　　I forget his name—
　　　　it's kind of crippled animal.
They bring that woman, and they dig quite a ways.
And they went underground till they reach her.
And they bring 'em back to that tunnel.
And they get 'em alive.
And they have her for a wife,
　　one of them.
And that is why, see, that one,
　　they come alive.
And maybe someone, they come alive just like that,
　　somewhere.
Not the same place.

One in Spences Bridge, that was a man.
He come alive.
And another one come alive.
And I think it was some more.
But I can't think of it now.
It was three that I know.
Come alive.
That's from Badger.
Because they doing it.
That's why.

PHONETIC

TRANSCRIPTIONS OF

OKANAGAN WORDS

These transcriptions were compiled with the assistance of University of British Columbia linguist Mandy Jimmie, in consultation with Dr. Anthony Mattina's *Colville-Okanagan Dictionary* (Occasional Papers in Linguistics, No. 5, Missoula: University of Montana, 1987).

Awk-MEEN	ʔax̣mín
chap-TEEK-whl	captíkʷɬ
ha-HA	x̣aʔx̣áʔ
HUSH-hush	xásxs
ko-RA-tin	kʷr'íʔtn
Kwee-LA-kin	kʷilákn
KWEELSH-tin	kʷ̓iḷstn
N-kli-kum-CHEEN	nX̣əX̣əmcín
plak	pɬax̣
Shash-ap-KANE	səsapqín
Shash-AP-kin	səsápkn
Shmit-KUN-tin	smitqə́ńtin
shnay-WHUM	snyxʷám
shoo-MISH	sumíx
Ya-kum-DI-kun	yaqəmtíkən

ACKNOWLEDGEMENTS

I would like to thank the Phillips Fund of the American Philosophical Society, Philadelphia, and the Canadian Ethnology Service of the Canadian Museum of Civilization, Hull, Quebec, for their funding of field research in 1981 and 1982, during which some of these stories were recorded. I also wish to thank Blanca Chester and Lynne Jorgesen for their assistance with the transcription of the stories. I especially appreciate Blanca's quick response to my urgent requests during a very hectic period in her life.

In the fall of 1985, photographer Robert Semeniuk spent two days in the Similkameen Valley with Harry. His photographs are a treasure, and I thank him for taking the time to do this. I also wish to thank linguist Mandy Jimmie for her assistance with the phonetic transcriptions. I thank Denise Bukowski for her work with the manuscript.

There are two people who have been extremely supportive and helpful throughout the preparation of this book. Barbara Pulling of Douglas & McIntyre edited the manuscript carefully, and I appreciate greatly her many thoughtful suggestions and her gentle way of prodding during deadlines. She also loved the manuscript, which made my work with her very enjoyable. In the same way, I wish to thank my husband, Michael M'Gonigle. He was with me often while I sat with Harry. As an environmentalist, he has long had, with me, a strong and abiding interest in nature power.

Finally, I wish to pay tribute to Harry. This book, like the first, is what Harry Robinson was all about. After the publication of *Write It on Your Heart,* we established a scholarship at the Keremeos Secondary School in his name. The scholarship, based on the book's royalties, goes annually to a Native student who shows a particularly strong interest in any aspect of his or her Native culture. The royalties from *Nature Power* will continue to go to this scholarship fund.

HARRY ROBINSON was a well-known and highly respected Native elder from the Similkameen Valley. His first collaboration with Wendy Wickwire, *Write It on Your Heart* (Talonbooks), was published three months before his death in 1990. The book was a critical and popular success, elevating Harry Robinson to a prominent place in Canada's literary community.

WENDY WICKWIRE is an ethnographer who has worked with the Native people of British Columbia's interior for more than a decade. She is the compiler and editor of *Write It on Your Heart* and the coauthor, with Michael M'Gonigle, of the highly acclaimed *Stein: The Way of the River* (Talonbooks).